A Generation Betrayed

❖

It's Time to Stop the Sexual Revolution

by   Randy Kirk

HUNTINGTON HOUSE PUBLISHERS

Huntington House Publishers
P.O. Box 53788
Lafayette, Louisiana 70505

Library of Congress Card Catalog Number 93-78889
ISBN 1-56384-054-5

Dedication

❖

To my wife Pamela, our daughters Christian and Brandy, and our son Brian. It is my intent through this work to protect them from future harm caused by the result of the sexual revolution.

In a world full of shadows, it is sometimes difficult for us to believe we can really make a difference. Sometimes our little light seems small indeed. Sometimes the darkness looks overwhelming. But throughout history the church has always shone as a community of light that cannot be quenched. In a thousand dim arenas of need around the world, *the light still shines in the darkness–and the darkness cannot extinguish it* . . .

Chuck Colson, *The Body*

Contents

❖

v

Acknowledgments

❖

I want to give heartfelt thanks to the following individuals who have contributed to the final outcome of this work. First are those who took the time to read the first draft in its entirety and to provide their honest comments; the book is substantially better for their effort: my loving wife, Pam; my brother and his wife, Gary and Julie Kirk; my sister, Judy; my mother, Phyllis Kirk; my partner, Terry Brown; the chairman of the deacons of my local church, Brad Jensen; my wife's aunt, Bettie Meyer; my mother-in-law, Ruby Thronbrugh; the president and executive director of Medical Institute for Sexual Health, Joe McIlhaney and Tom Smith; policy consultant for Capitol Resource Institute, Natalie Williams; co-founder of Teen Aid, LeAnna Benn; founder of the National Association for Abstinence Education, Jo Ann Gasper. In addition, my thanks go to many who read parts of the work but especially my daughter, Christian Kirk, for her excellent help in the chapters for teen-agers, and Tom and Sharon Nichols. Finally, I would like to thank Huntington House for its amazing agreement to publish this book within three-and-a-half months from contract, and for the sweet spirit that permeates their organization.

One Victim's Story

❖

She struggled to focus her big, brown eyes. Even at two days old, that was the first thing you noticed about her. The eyelashes were next, black as night and so long they seemed to float in the air as she opened and closed those memorable eyes in newborn wonderment. Mom and dad agreed—they'd done well. Their baby was especially beautiful.

She was conceived out of wedlock, but by 1960 that was becoming less and less of a social stigma among the sophisticated set. Married now, her parents were excited and proud of their little girl. Like so many dads and moms before and since, they hoped they would have what it took to bring her up right.

Her life was pretty uneventful for the first eleven or so years. Her dad was in construction in Southern California, his union scale wages allowing the young family to live the suburban dream. Mom stayed home and took care of the house and kids. Dad worked hard and liked to hoist a few with the boys after work.

The little girl with the big, brown eyes and the long, black eyelashes was joined just fourteen months later by a sister who would be her source of torment (after all, isn't that a younger sister's job?) and later her best friend. Blessed with good looks, good grades, and good friends, she and her sister even inherited their mother's vocal talents and entered competitions as a team. She explains in her own words:

"I don't remember a lot about these early years. I think I was happy, although I was quiet and moody. My mom says I was sad. I know I had several close friends and did well in

school. I certainly don't remember thinking that my family
was any different than anybody else's. I wish I could remember more. One thing I can remember vividly was the night
my mom, my sister, and I walked across the big field near
where we lived with just a few belongings. Mom and Dad
were fighting. We stayed in a hotel and wondered what
would become of us. I was very scared."

There was more than a normal amount of strain in the
marriage. As the girls grew up, the signs of trouble became
more and more evident. Finally, there was a major rift.
"There was one separation. I think it was for about four
months or so. At about this same time, I began to question
my dad's faithfulness to my mom. Then, when I was around
the age of eleven or twelve, he had an affair and had me talk
to his lover on the phone. He went on to explain that she
had two boys. I remember feeling very hurt because he was
playing dad to kids that weren't even his."

A final desperate effort was made to save the marriage.
During the separation, however, the suburban home had
been sold. Now, with dad back, the family moved into an
apartment near the beach in Santa Monica. It seemed like a
good place to start over. It wasn't. They were only blocks
from one of the most famous of the hippie hangouts, Venice,
California.

There was no way to avoid exposing this impressionable
preteen to vagrants, prostitutes, drug addicts, and dropouts.
She was lonely, scared, and angry at being uprooted from
her home, friends, and neighborhood. She was relieved and
satisfied to have a group of people who cared for her, since
she didn't feel that much love at home. The behavior patterns of her new group became her own behavior patterns.
She figured that it only made sense that if those who seemed
to care most about her behaved a certain way, she should
want to be a part of that.

"When my parents got back together we moved to Santa
Monica to make a new start. It was so hard to leave my old
school and friends, especially with our home life being so
uncertain. I made new friends right away. I wish I'd waited
longer. It is pretty clear to me that the group I hung out with
at this time set the stage for the horrors that were to come."

Her mom and dad thought the seventies were "far out"—especially her dad. The marriage grew shakier and shakier as each year passed. While dad was enjoying the best that the seventies had to offer, a now fourteen-year-old girl with big, brown eyes needed him. He seemed to know that he wasn't giving her all she needed, so he tried to make up for it by being "one of the gang." Any discipline that mom provided was countered by dad's permissiveness. "I remember knowing by this time that things weren't going that well for my parents. I was torn by my father's actions. I wanted his love, and I wanted him to give me the things (like cigarettes) that my mom wouldn't allow. At the same time, I wanted him to be my dad, not another one of my friends. I looked to him for guidance and discipline. Instead, he came to us looking for approval."

"Please understand, I don't blame my dad for what follows, at least not all the time. A great deal of what happened was a product of our times. Could my dad have prevented what happened? Maybe. But he was a product of those times too."

It started with cigarettes at thirteen. Sex entered the picture at fourteen. By fifteen there was alcohol and marijuana. Skipping school was an unfortunate side effect of alcohol, marijuana, and sex. The precious jewel that had melted her daddy's heart only fourteen years ago was now a badly troubled adolescent.

"My friends and the things they did were much better than school and home. We lived near the beach, and it's pretty easy to become invisible down there. I thought this new life was great. I liked the cigarettes and beer and marijuana, and I wanted everybody in the group to see that I was one of them. I especially wanted the attention of the boys. I can remember how special I felt at eleven when I got my first kiss. I felt like a queen. I felt so special that this boy would choose me to give me my first kiss.

"I started having sex when I was in the eighth grade. When this boy wanted to go further I felt more 'grown-up.' At first I think I became sexually active as a way of being accepted by my boyfriend. I also thought if I didn't give in he wouldn't like me anymore. I had friends who were sexually experienced. I wanted to be like those who were active and be seen as better than those who weren't.

"Much later in my life I realized that I was definitely trying to replace the attention I lacked from my dad. I thought that I liked sex, but as time went on and I had encounters with many different men, it didn't really mean anything. It wasn't special."

Her parents' marriage relationship didn't get any better, nor did the little girl's relationship with her parents. "I hated being at home. I felt it was the worst place to be. My mom and I fought. My dad and I didn't connect at all. He didn't show any concern or love. I realize he loved me, but he wasn't there for me emotionally."

By fourteen she became known to the police as a runaway. After one such incident at age fifteen, her mom in desperation agreed to have her spend a week in a mental health facility at a local hospital; a family counselor had advised her mother that might deter her from running away. It was here that she met the man (a twenty-year-old paranoid-schizophrenic and alcoholic) who would father her first child.

At fifteen she was pregnant, and the father absent.

"When I found out I was pregnant, I was excited. Now I would have my own family. The future was clear. My boyfriend would marry me, and my baby would love me. Besides, I would be out of my parents' house. That dream didn't last long. During the seventh month of the pregnancy, my boyfriend took a trip across the country where he got involved with another girl. A few weeks later he tried to make up, but I wasn't interested."

She was sent to a home for pregnant girls in hopes that this change of environment would be beneficial. The mother-to-be never thought twice about whether to keep the baby. It was only 1975; abortion was still considered to be murder by most. "I knew about abortion but never considered it. My mom wanted me to give the baby up for adoption. I told her that there was no way I was going to carry a baby for nine months just to hand it over to somebody else. I don't think there was ever a time where I seriously thought of any option other than keeping my baby." At the ripe old age of sixteen, the little child-mother with the big, brown eyes gave birth to a beautiful daughter with big, hazel eyes and long, brown eyelashes. She had been born out of wedlock (and by 1976 this was of little concern to anyone). Single motherhood was a somewhat new phenomenon then, but not considered a very big deal. I didn't have a clue. What now? I didn't know anything about taking care of a baby. I couldn't work. My mom and dad were near divorce, so I was practically alone. My sister was only fifteen at the time. Of course, I was a woman now, a mother. So during the brief time I stayed with my parents, I thought mom was unreasonable to insist on restrictions to my freedom. As soon as I found a job, I moved out on my own with my new baby.

"When the baby was about four months old, I got involved with a new boyfriend. He set a pattern that would repeat over and over. As each new man came into our lives, I fantasized that he would be the father for our little family. He would love my little girl like she was his own and take care of us. In this fantasy, we would have more kids and live happily ever after."

A seventeen-year-old girl living with her boyfriend and a baby in 1977 was a recipe for trouble. Parties, alcohol, and drugs competed for time with baby, job, and housework. And these years were more stable than those that were to come. "I was a kid, and I wanted to do what the other kids were doing. I also needed a man in my life, and as I look back today, I wasn't very particular about who it was. I felt that *they* (the men) would make me happy. *They* would make me feel like the person I wanted to be. *They* would treat me special and want to have a family with me." But these boys and men didn't stay and build a home. They left when they got what they wanted or wanted something new. The little mom was headed straight downhill on the emotional roller coaster of life.

"Most of the time I would just cry and cry in total despair. I couldn't understand why they didn't want me anymore. What did I do to cause them to leave me? That was a question I commonly asked myself. I always felt that it was my fault. I felt my self-esteem sink lower and lower each time I experienced a break-up. The only thing that could repair my broken heart and lack of self-worth was another man."

With her life a shambles and easy access to drugs, the obvious happened. "Drugs were a central part of my life. In fact, I guess my life revolved around drugs. They gave me courage. I felt that I could really express myself when I was high. If someone criticized me later for something I said, I could blame it on the drugs. I can't really say whether I was physically addicted since I didn't try to give them up. I didn't want to give them up."

It was during this time that one man began to play a bigger and bigger part in her life. They had many things in common. They both liked drugs, alcohol, and partying. "He wasn't much different from the rest. He stayed around. I knew he was sleeping with other women. Sometimes I would punish him by sleeping with other men. I don't know if he knew I did or not, or if he would have cared had he known. Most of the other relationships ended when I increased the pressure for a commitment. I certainly pushed for one in his case too. Sometimes he would seem to agree. Other times he seemed to know I wasn't going to follow through on any threats to break up if there was no commitment."

Soon the three had become a "family." The little girl called him Dad. There was no commitment or marriage, but it was pretty close to stability. Clearly, however, the fire they were playing with was going to burn them. "We didn't use birth control of any kind. Nobody used condoms. We all agreed they ruined sex. Some of my friends were on the pill, but most weren't. I didn't want to become pregnant. In fact, I was worried that I would. We didn't live with the reality of birth control. Every month I anxiously waited for my period.

"Anyway, the inevitable happened. I was upset and knew he would be. I wanted to go through with the pregnancy, but he didn't. He made it very clear that he did not want to be a father or have that responsibility. He also made it clear that if I went through with the pregnancy, he would not stick around.

"I knew abortion was wrong. I did not want to do that to the life that was within me. But I also didn't want to be alone, and I felt I had to go through with it or I'd lose him. At the time I shoved my feelings deep inside and just ignored them."

There would be a second abortion prior to the birth of her second little girl. "I cried and cried the second time. He even almost agreed to have the baby. I was so upset. He was with me when I did it, but he couldn't possibly understand the pain I was going through. When I got pregnant the third time, I put my foot down. Coincidently, I had recently felt a little more powerful in the relationship. I was interested in another man and suggested that we both date other people. He didn't like that idea a bit and asked me to marry him. We started making plans and that's when I found out I was pregnant again.

"With my new feelings of power, I pushed my position all the way. I told him I was having this baby, with or without him. This is the first time I can ever remember feeling like I was in charge of my own destiny. We were married and his Dutch ancestry gave us a fair-haired cutie."

No one could doubt that this second little girl's complexion and hair coloring came from daddy, but the big, brown eyes surely were passed on from mom. Now age twenty-two, the subject of our story had seen her dream turn into reality. Married with a family, here was her chance for a stable life. Quickly, however, the dream turned to a nightmare.

"My husband was a trucker. I'm sure there are truckers who are faithful to their wives. I was sure he wasn't. We were still into the drug scene. When he was home, we partied. There was very little about the relationship that could be considered good before we got married. Getting married didn't help anything.

"I became pregnant again. I tried to assert my power again. Unfortunately, he felt safe now that we were married and threatened to leave the girls and me if I didn't have an abortion. At the time I couldn't see any options that didn't include him."

The marriage ended on the second anniversary. The following year would be the worst. With her self-esteem at its lowest ever, drugs, alcohol, and the search for a male companion totally dominated her life. Her cocaine use so controlled her that her family convinced her to put the girls in foster care. They feared that the kids weren't getting proper care. They also anticipated the worst: the girls, ages eight and two, coming home from day care to find their mommy dead from an overdose. Much of the time she didn't have her own apartment and stayed with different friends one night at a time. Her life consisted of bar-hopping and one-night stands.

"Then it happened. I thought I had really met the perfect guy. He was good-looking, charming, and financially well off. He was a drug dealer; therefore, I could be assured of a supply. My fantasy life was full of my plans to marry him. He had given me a ring. And all this was within the first two weeks after we met.

"By the end of our fourth week together, the relationship was already turning sour. He dumped me. I didn't find out until a week later that I was pregnant. I told him about my condition. He thought it was a ploy to get him back. Then I did use the offer of an abortion to try to get money from him. However, since it was totally my choice this time, I would never have actually aborted the baby. He denied his responsibility and said that if I really was pregnant, it wasn't his."

Faced with her sixth pregnancy, two girls to care for, and a serious drug and alcohol problem, this twenty-four-year-old woman with big, brown eyes was at a crossroads. The next two weeks were to offer proof of the real character that had lain dormant for these eight long years. "I was at the bottom. I tried more drugs and alcohol one night, went to my mother's therapist another night, and turned to friends for comfort. Then I decided to go to church. I had been in and out of church all during this period. I had even been baptized. But my earlier experiences had failed to reach my heart. I just kept sliding back into a lifestyle that seemed to offer more, but didn't.

"Two weeks after the paternity discussion, I attended a revival at the church my mom attended. I had been off drugs for several days. I went forward and asked Jesus to come into my life and meant it. He did. The pastor told my mother, 'You have your daughter back.'"

"It would be a fairy tale to say that this was the end of struggles in this new believer's life. Even Christians have to endure difficulties. It would be six long months before she could afford to bring her girls back home. "The girls were living with a family from my church until I could afford to get a place for us all to live. It was horrible leaving my babies after visiting with them for an evening or a weekend. They would hang onto me, crying, not wanting me to go. At times they would ask me when we would be able to live together again. It hurt me when they asked because I couldn't give them a definite answer.

"At this same time, my mom and I began discussing the idea of getting a house and living together. We would share living expenses. This way the girls could come back to me. We found a modest home that was within our budget and were finally able to reunite. The best part of the whole thing was God's timing in putting us back together. We became a family again on Mother's Day."

Even as she began to see improvements in almost every area of her life, there was still the question of the pregnancy. "I knew from the start that it would not be fair to my new baby or to the girls that I try to raise a third child. I also knew that this time, since the choice would be mine, I would definitely have this baby. This left only one option, and that was adoption.

"You can make that decision and know it's the right one. You can even be totally committed to it and see it as the only possible solution. But as that little person grows and kicks and squirms inside of you, there is no way to avoid dreaming about how to keep your baby. Part of my new way of life, however, was to give up all my vices. That included men. I had decided that I would not date again until I met the man that God intended for me to marry. Without the help of a husband, the idea of my supporting three kids was out of the question."

The little baby's time came to join the world. The selection of the new parents had been made just a couple of days before the birth day. They were a sweet couple, and best of all, they shared her faith.

"The delivery went smoothly, and I delivered a beautiful baby boy. I was his mom for two days. I fed him and changed his diapers. I looked at his tiny fingers and toes. I smelled him and kissed him. I sang to him and held him close to me.

And then I changed my mind. I told my sister I couldn't let him go. I cried and cried and gave every argument as to why I should keep him.

"My mom came to the rescue. She showed me how he would be much better off with someone who could take care of him. He would be better off in a stable home with a dad and a mom. She also said that my girls needed everything I could give them. I knew she was right, and I reluctantly went through with the adoption. The night that I relinquished him was the hardest thing I ever had to go through. I went to the adoption agency with the baby and the social worker. It was there that I handed the baby over to the adoptive parents. All I wanted to do was cry as they took him and walked away with him. But I didn't, because I wanted them to see that I was strong. I was quiet all the way home because if I had said one word, I would have lost it.

"That night as I thought over what I had done, I just let my emotions go and cried the whole evening. I called one of the deaconesses from my church, seeking comfort. She told me that God had a plan for me and that I needed to turn to His Word to find my peace. She told me to read Isaiah 41:10: 'Fear thou not; for I am with thee: be not dismayed; for I am thy God: I will strengthen thee; yea, I will help thee; yea, I will uphold thee with the right hand of my righteousness.' I cried myself to sleep that night, but when I awoke the following morning, I found that I was totally at peace with my decision and knew that I would never feel pained about it again."

In the months that followed, life became almost normal. She became concerned about paying the light bill, not the drug bill. She spent her time taking care of little girls, not looking for men. Life was the best it had been in years. "My healing was not without bumps in the road. I wasn't actively looking for a man to complete my life, but I was very much aware of this missing part of me. I would ask God why he was taking so long to give me a husband. Sometimes I felt that maybe I would never find a partner." One night in church, she shared part of this story with a man she had met a few weeks before. He later told her that he had been "blown away" by what she had experienced and suggested that he would be interested in helping her turn the story into a book. He said he saw the potential in her amazing life for its power as a witness to the hope that is available through faith. He suggested it might also be a way to supplement her meager income. "I was excited, but also very skeptical about the idea. We wrote up a contract. I asked my mom to meet with this man. He was a businessman and had written some business books and articles. My mom felt comfortable about the deal, and we agreed to do it.

"Over the next several months, I wrote down all I could remember. He read what I had finished, encouraged me, and gave advice. Sometimes the advice went beyond the book. He helped me with my budget, my kids, and other aspects of my growth. He was struggling a bit, too. His wife of seventeen years had decided she wasn't in love with him anymore. They were both in counseling. He was doing every-thing he knew to keep the marriage together. He told me some of the details, and I offered him ideas as to what might work to win her back. I even recommended my therapist.

"Looking back, it's amazing that this relationship didn't get messy. He had problems at home; I was really needy. But we couldn't have been more proper. Maybe that's because I needed to be good. Also, because of his personality, it would have been very surprising if he had made any passes at me."

It wasn't that difficult for these two to maintain the proper distance. Because of their individual situations, they couldn't even consider each other in any other way but as friends and business partners.

"His wife didn't attend church with him. Sometimes we would use the time right after church to discuss the book. On one such Sunday we went to a local restaurant to work on the book over lunch. As we waited for the meal, he told me that he and his wife had made a final decision to split up. She just had no interest in making the marriage work again." He felt strongly that marriage is a lifetime contract for better or worse. He was willing to endure while his wife "worked out" her issues. But in California it only takes one to make a divorce.

This change in the situation caused new light to fall on the relationship. It was as if they saw each other for the first

time. A whirlwind courtship followed. She and her friend
were married in a big church wedding with family and friends
all around. Her dad gave her away. Her mother cried. She
still has those big, brown eyes and the long, black eyelashes
that seem to float in air as she opens and closes them. Her
name is Pamela. I was the author/businessman. She is my
wife, and we have been married for six years. I adopted the
girls, Christian, now 16, and Brandy, now 11. Their mother,
Pamela, and I planned the next addition to our family.

Pam: "It was sure a new experience for me. We decided
that we should wait at least two years to have a baby so that
Randy could devote his full attention to the girls and me.
Once we felt comfortable that we were functioning as a
family, then it would be time for expansion."

Randy: "My first wife didn't want children; I did. While
we never argued over this, it might still have been an under-
lying reason for our eventual break-up. Having these two
little girls to take care of was like heaven on earth to me.
Planning another life was just as new to me as it was to Pam."

Pam: "How different it was to go through a pregnancy
knowing that you are loved and that your husband is totally
committed to you for the rest of your life. Our little boy,
Brian, was born four years ago. God gave me a great gift
with him. Remember, the baby I had given up for adoption
was a boy."

Randy: "It should come as no surprise that Brian has big,
hazel eyes and very, very long eyelashes. I know this story to
be true in all of its details. I have lived through Pam's learning how to overcome those horrible eight years. Her friends
today know her as chairwoman of the nursery committee or
one of the leaders of the three- and four-year-olds' program,
but everyone is amazed when she gives her testimony.

Pam's story is part of the reason I have undertaken this
book. Think about her testimony as you read the following
chapters. Think about the numbers of girls who are going
through similar circumstances—and much worse—right this
very minute. Think about how many of them will never
experience a real marriage, attend church, or raise their kids
in a beautiful, lovingly managed home. Think how many of
them will become sterile, live a lifetime of pain or discom-

fort, or die as the result of a sexually transmitted disease. Think how many will die from drugs or spend their life with one or more abusive men. Finally, think how many more may be eaten away by the emotional and physical poisons of alcohol or end their lives through suicide. For this little girl, it all started when she was barely a teen, and she thought it was O.K. to have sex, because "everybody did. . . . "

Two

The Sexual Revolution

❖

No man in modern times has shaped public attitudes . . . of human sexuality more than the late Alfred C. Kinsey. He advocated that all sexual behaviors considered deviant were normal, . . . Few people realize that the data he presented were not . . . scientific. . . . In addition to being highly biased, Kinsey's results may have been fraudulent.

Kinsey, Sex, and Fraud
by Dr. Judith A. Reisman and Edward W. Eichel

What have we done?! How is it possible in one generation to so completely turn reason on its head? Where did we go wrong? Can it really be true that intelligent, well-meaning adults are encouraging teen-age girls and young women to pass themselves around like a bowl of picked over fruit? How can it be? Fathers and mothers of these youngsters sit idly by while television, movies, and radio teach them about the glories of sex without love or commitment. Where are our leaders? Will no one stand up against this craziness? Will no one say "STOP!"?

Between 1948 and 1953 a war-weary America was introduced to a whole new way of thinking about our sexual selves. Alfred C. Kinsey published the results of his research in two amazing books, *Sexual Behavior in the Human Male* and *Sexual Behavior in the Human Female*. Though it seems likely now that much of Kinsey's research was flawed, if not fraudulent, the impact of his reports cannot be understated.

Kinsey was the founder of the Sexual Revolution. Contending that Americans were not nearly so prudish as most believed, Kinsey proposed that large numbers of us were engaging in premarital and extra-marital sex. Up until that time and through the early sixties, sex outside of marriage was considered to be not only abnormal, but "just not done." At the very most, society accepted the idea that some young men would sow their wild oats with "those kind of girls." Slowly, but surely, however, the veil of statistics offered by Kinsey began to overcome our personal observation of reality. We didn't know anybody who was having an affair, but scientists said half of us were. As we looked at our neighbors it seemed improbable, but maybe there was more going on than we knew about. As the media and the textbooks repeated over and over again the findings of Kinsey and those who followed, our culture soon began to question its own eyes, ears, and thinking. If so many are engaged in this activity, we were encouraged to ask ourselves, how can it be called abnormal? If not abnormal, then surely we can rationalize away its being immoral. If not immoral or abnormal, "What could be the harm?" This insidious phrase became the battle cry of those who desired a brave new world of "anything goes" sexuality.

What could be the harm? What a tragic question that has become. Let's start a list of the harms: (1) Over 30 million aborted babies. Even those who favor unlimited access to the procedure of abortion, do not fail to see 1.5 million abortions per year as anything but a deplorable situation. (2) Millions of women who have aborted those 30 million babies suffering the emotional aftermath. Usually, they are alone in their grief, unable or unwilling to share their burden for fear of the reaction from friends and family. (3) More millions of babies born to mothers who are not ready to care for them, often resent them, and commonly don't want them. (4) Countless millions of cases of venereal disease resulting in pain, discomfort, disfigurement, disability, infertility, and even death. Remember, all of these potential harms existed prior to the appearance of AIDS. (5) Ever increasing millions of women living in poverty with one or more illegitimate children, no man present in the home, with only poverty and desperation to look forward to. (6) An entire generation of teen-age girls facing the constant rejection of young men who date them only until they succumb to the pressure to have sex. Consider the irony of the women's movement seeking to build every woman's concept of self while at the same time promoting the disaster of sexual liberation. (7) Countless magazines, photos, newspapers, motion pictures, audio and video tapes, and records devoted to degrading women as sexual objects to be used, abused, raped, beaten up, tortured, and even murdered. (8) Our young women stressed out over what a date might try, what is expected of them, and what might be the awful consequences of the wrong decision; this instead of using such an evening to enjoy learning about each other's hopes, dreams, and feelings. (9) Relationships between parents and children ruined because of the tragedy of teen pregnancy. (10) Otherwise sound marriages destroyed by infidelity. (11) Romances destroyed because she wouldn't, or because she did and he's no longer interested. (12) Young girls turning to alcohol, drugs, or suicide to overcome the loneliness. (13) Government, business, and religious leaders dethroned by their sexual exploits. (14) Our mothers, wives, and daughters assaulted, raped, tortured, or killed by men whose actions have been scripted by pornography. (15) Marriages destroyed and children of those broken marriages damaged by lack of commitment, respect, and responsibility. (16) Millions of youngsters wanting to know "Who's my daddy?" (17) More millions wanting to know "Why doesn't daddy live with us? (18) So many more wondering when mommy will leave. After all, "Daddy left, and he loved us, didn't he?" (19) Millions of children living in poverty, dependent upon the welfare state, because there's no daddy in the picture. (20) More millions of children passed from family member to family member, then to foster care, nights in the county's care, and days in the courtrooms. (21) Babies and children enduring physical, emotional, and sexual abuse by step-parents, foster parents, live-in boyfriends and girlfriends, and one-night stands. (22) Teen-agers echoing their upbringing through early pregnancy, alcohol or drug abuse, and dependence on welfare. (23) Too many teen-agers reaching out to gangs for nurture and support that they can't get at home. The gang becomes their substitute family. (24) So many young women reaching out to any man who'll have them, hold them, and hopefully love them. Each of these men become a substitute dad for as long as they will stay.

What could be the harm? Surely no one dreamed of these consequences at the time. There is no grand conspiracy afoot to destroy America and much more of the rest of the civilized world through sexual promiscuity. Each and every one of us must face up to the responsibility for what has happened. Were too many of us asleep on our watch?

Even if many or most of us would accept our part in making this mess, there are those who are yet to be convinced that anything is wrong. If a few scientists were to predict the end of life as we know it because of greenhouse gases, acid rain, ozone depletion, a coming ice age, pesticides, or red meat the headlines would quickly turn theory into fact. But I guess the horrible consequences of our current sexual practices are just not news. Where are the headlines bemoaning the staggering number of cases of sexually transmitted diseases among our teens and young adults? Why haven't *Time* and *Newsweek* devoted cover stories to the real reasons behind increasing poverty rates in America among families headed by single mothers? Are there too many people making a living off our depravity to allow us to turn toward a better way of living? Are there too many among our leaders who are themselves so corrupted by their need for sex without limits or responsibility that they can't risk sacrificing their lifestyle in order to promote a greater good?

I have one question for those who can't see the need to advance to a time of sexual responsibility and morality: What in the world have we, as individuals or as a society, gained by the sexual revolution? The losses are so clear. Where, pray tell, are the benefits?

Today, I am declaring an end to the sexual revolution! It is never easy to move a people to give up something they might currently enjoy in order to gain a greater good, but it must be done. And it must be done now. In later chapters, I will propose specific ways that we can work as individuals and as a nation to bring about such change. First, however, we must lay more groundwork.

Three

Who Gains from Sexual Liberation? Who Loses?

❖

We can't have it both ways. We can't laugh at modesty and wink at chastity and then expect boys to show a respectful attitude towards girls. We can't desensitize students and then expect them to grow up to be sensitive spouses.

Orange County Register,
Don Feder quoting Bill Kilpatrick, Boston College
education professor and author of
Why Johnny Can't Tell Right from Wrong

It is difficult to imagine that anyone truly gains from the premise that illicit and promiscuous sex should be a prominent part of our society. It is equally difficult to imagine that anyone benefits from engaging in sexual promiscuity before, between, or during marriage. However, let's first take a look at some groups who at least appear to benefit or believe they or others do.

Certainly there are those who gain financially from the exploitation of women and men by appealing to their worst instincts. Thus the pornographers, both hard and soft core, make millions from the distribution of films, magazines, and videos. Producers of television programs also seem to believe they can gain ratings (which translate into fame and money) if they constantly push the edge of acceptability.

Those who make products or offer services related to the sexual encounter also stand to make a financial gain.

This might include manufacturers of birth control devices, love "toys," and "how to" sex books. It would also benefit those who treat sexually transmitted diseases and those who destroy the new life produced by sexual behavior (a baby) through abortion. Then there are the thousands who provide services, such as Planned Parenthood, for the "perpetrators" and the innocent victims listed in the previous chapter.

Another large group of beneficiaries would be those who produce entertainment for and advertise in the media. Not too long ago, even those with the most sexually liberal attitudes criticized advertisers for their portrayal of women as sex objects. The social critics of those times believed it was somehow wrong to use sex to sell. Now many of those same voices are silent as we use sex to sell PG movies, teen-age music, MTV, or Friday night "kids" programming. Advertisers who exploit women or sexual appetites believe they are gaining from this approach. In addition to businesses who advertise in these media, we would include TV stations, networks, and production companies among those also gaining financial benefits from sexual exploitation.

The group which appears to benefit the most from all of this "free" sex is men. If a young girl or woman is willing to offer herself sexually to a man without asking for a commitment in return, he will ordinarily take her up on the offer. Men therefore gain in the sense that they can now find a new sexual partner with little effort, expense, or other long-term cost. These men are also potential victims of sexually transmitted diseases (STDs), but the threat to men is far less than that for women. (The exception is AIDS, of course. However, since less than three percent of the current carriers of the HIV virus are women, the odds of a man contracting AIDS through heterosexual activity is very low.) Other STDs are either exclusively dangerous to women or have consequences that result in much greater suffering for the fair sex. (For a detailed discussion of the consequences of STDs, see the chapter entitled, "An Urgent Appeal to Teen-age Girls.")

Men also see gain in that they are much more interested in visually stimulating sexual materials, most becoming quite stimulated by the mere sight of nude women or even parts of women. The excitement is elevated if the woman is dancing, touching herself, or engaged in sexual activity with a man or another woman. For many men, they are further titillated if the pictured women are young or children. Finally, some enjoy materials that depict women hurt, tortured, or even murdered. Therefore, to the extent that this material is readily available, men would appear to gain. For little or no money, without fear of arrest or ridicule, and generally with no inconvenience, men today are able to indulge their wildest fantasies. A large percentage of men alive today have taken advantage of the availability of sexually "free" women or sexually erotic materials.

Some women could be thought to gain from the sexual revolution. First there are those who philosophically believe women should have the same standing as men to enjoy unfettered, unfeeling sex. They would ask, "Why shouldn't we be able to love 'em and leave 'em? Why shouldn't we be able to enjoy the physical side of sex without having to tie ourselves to any one man emotionally? Why shouldn't we be able to sow our wild oats? Why shouldn't we use men the way they use us?"

Most women are sexually stimulated by watching, listening to, or reading about romantic goings-on between two lovers. This is undoubtedly enhanced for some as the subject becomes steamier and steamier. Women are just as prone as men to be drawn by this material to desire sexual activities. Thus, one could argue that some women feel they have gained from the availability of highly erotic romance novels, sexually explicit movies and videos, and ever-more-daring soap operas and TV programs.

Other women would claim that they gained through "catching" their future husband as a result of their sexual prowess or by purposely becoming pregnant with a man who would do the "honorable" thing. Still others claim that they enjoy sex within marriage more because of their experience with sex outside of marriage. Some have even proposed that their entire marriage has been enhanced by extramarital sex with, or without, their husband's knowledge or participation.

There are those who believe that women must be able to act like men sexually in order to compete with them eco-

nomically. If men feel they can have sex without commitment or feeling, but women feel compelled to find sexual
outlets only within the confines of marriage, women are at
a disadvantage. If one were to buy this argument, which is
questionable at best, we would next propose that any means
to an end is worthy. The logical extension would be that
women would use men sexually to advance their careers, or
marry young men as trophy husbands. Wouldn't society be
better off to bring men who act without scruples up to the
standards of our women, than to drag women down to the
level of such men?

In order to be certain to bring every possible beneficiary
to the table, let's include children. There is a very common
belief that our openness about sexuality helps our children
to be less uptight about the subject when they reach adulthood. In a similar vein, the entire adult population can
throw off any guilt or anxiety they might have felt in an
earlier time over divorce, promiscuity, abortion, lewd behavior, or adultery. Since each of these become mere lifestyle
choices, there is no reason to think twice about doing them.
This is why the concept is called liberation. We are free to
do anything we please in the sexual arena. This is especially
true since, with this type of thinking, what we do in the
privacy of our bedroom is none of society's business and
hurts no one.

Now that we have listed the "winners" of the sexual
revolution, let's next take a very close look at the losers. At
the top of the list, without a doubt, are the women.

I grew up at the very end of the period that preceded the
sexual revolution. I fix the transition year as 1966, the year
I graduated from high school. Sure, many in presexual revo-
lutionary America were experimenting with the new morality prior to 1966, and there were many who by chance of
culture or geography didn't participate in the new way of life
until later, if at all. However, I can only too easily recall that
girls who "did it" when I was in high school were not considered marrying material. Even those who would allow a
boy to "feel them up" were suspect. Those who became
pregnant were not looked upon kindly by either the kids or
the culture. In 1967, a debate topic in the debating society

questioned whether living together prior to marriage was a good idea. In order to evaluate this approach, we had to look at more liberal European communities such as Sweden, because there was virtually no statistical data available in America about couples living together without the benefit of a marriage certificate.

I considered myself lucky during my dating career to receive a chaste kiss at the end of a first date with a "good" girl. Virginity among unmarried teen-age girls and young women was prized, not scorned. Certainly a double standard existed in those days. Most boys were expected to get whatever they could from a girl. Not everyone condoned sexual experimentation by boys; however, a certain amount of sexual "experience" has been accepted for young men through almost all of recorded history. If a teen-age boy didn't seek sexual union he would be the subject of harassment in the locker room. Many young men grossly exaggerated or even fabricated sexual exploits in order to avoid this ribbing.

Almost every school had one or two girls who were known to be "easy." Boys who were inclined to sow their wild oats would seek out these promiscuous girls or visit professional prostitutes to gain their stripes. Boys did not take out the "good girls" to have sex. This is the overriding difference between then and now. Boys respected the latter too much to try anything. These girls respected themselves too much to allow even the pushiest boys to get away with anything.

Today, most young men see most girls and women as "wanting sex." There is no respect on either side of the equation—these women have no respect for the men, either. Moreover, this mutual lack of respect translates into lack of self-respect. Allow me to interrupt this train of thought for just a moment to anticipate my critics. Those who think they are the winners in the sex-for-free era may review my discussion of how it used to be and say they remember it differently. They will say there were good girls they knew of who "did it." They'll point to boys they knew during that time who had less interest in women who didn't sleep around than in those who did. I maintain only that the general rule before the late sixties was that women got married, had sex, got pregnant, and had babies—in that order. Since that time, it has become more common for teen-age girls to have sex, get pregnant, maybe get married, and have babies or abortions, without regard to order.

Regardless of the exceptions then or now, the reality remains: today's young men do not respect their female peers. Today, the situation is completely upside-down. Young men frequently date only those girls who are known to sleep around. Teen-age girls who remain virgins are laughed at by their girlfriends. Young women are considered totally "out of it" if they have yet to sleep with a man. In fact, the more the better. Let's take a look at the typical dating career of our girls today.

First date. For the younger teen it may be with another couple or a day at the beach or park, but most parents today are quite willing to allow their young daughters to be in unescorted places with their boyfriends. The older teen will generally be going out in a car, alone with the boy. The boy will almost certainly move quickly to hand-holding, kissing (which today is primarily "French" or erotic kissing), and possibly some fondling. If the boy doesn't start it, the girl likely will. If the girl resists the boy's advances he may wait until the next date or he may become quite aggressive. If on the other hand, the girl encourages his actions at all, he will likely push forward as quickly and as far as she will allow. Again, she may even be the aggressive one. (This aggressiveness is commonly the result of her feeling that this is the only way she can attract the boy.)

Second date. The entire time is devoted to exploring sexual issues. One or both push for more experimentation. Talk of where they can find more privacy is about the only talk that takes place. If the girl resisted on the first date, the boy will use all of his wiles to push the sexual part of the relationship along on this date. He will explain how much he loves her, how they will always be together, and how everyone does "it." If she still resists, he is forced to do the unthinkable: decide if he really likes her as a person, not as a sex machine. For many young men this will be the last date if she doesn't at least offer hope of feeding his sexual needs. For another smaller percentage, they might decide to use force.

Third date. Depending on the age and sexual experience of the boy (and to a lesser extent the girl), the heat will be turned up on this and each subsequent outing. There could be a period of weeks or even months before the young couple engage in actual intercourse. This period will be taken up with various kinds of "outercourse" (as it is now called), including petting, mutual masturbation, and/or oral sex.

Anyone who believes that outersex will serve as a substitute for intercourse over more than a few weeks or months has not had personal experience with the matter.

After the couple has sex once or a few times, the boy will begin to lose interest, even as the girl becomes more and more dependent upon the love and closeness she feels. As he loses interest, she becomes ever more clingy, which causes him to lose both respect and interest. The relationship ends with the young girl thinking her life is over. She will feel somehow responsible. She will believe that she was not pretty, slim, clever, or sexy enough. Her very frequent reaction will be to immediately seek reassurance of her value through a new relationship. However, this time, she will move much more aggressively toward consummation of the sexual part of the relationship, believing that she can hold on to the new boyfriend by keeping him satisfied sexually.

What bitter irony it is that this very act of giving in to the boyfriend's sexual drive is the reason that most young (and older) men end the relationship. They enjoy the chase, the challenge. Once having achieved the top prize, the intrigue goes out of the game. He is off, after a new challenge, and the pattern now repeats itself.

First, there is the search for a partner, any partner, to provide the love and attention the girl needs so desperately in order to continue to believe she is worthwhile. Then, she fights to hold on to the new boyfriend by offering him whatever he demands sexually. Again, the boy loses interest and the young lady is left feeling even more unlovable. Her self-image is further damaged as she reflects on her own lack of morality.

At this point the young woman is very likely to turn to drink, drugs, or suicide as the pain of rejection and guilt become too hard to deal with. With all of this comes the increased chance of pregnancy. These men don't want to use "protection." She doesn't want him to leave, so she isn't going to insist on any form of birth control, including condoms. Here you have the primary reason for condom failure in the prevention of pregnancy or disease transmission: they aren't used.

If our young lady takes the pill, there is still a substantial chance of contracting a sexually transmitted disease (STD). Three million teen-agers are infected annually with one or more of twenty-five different STDs. If only this were the end of the list of how our young women are big losers in this age of the new morality. It certainly isn't.

Tens of thousands are being assaulted each year through rape; there are so many rapes now that we have begun to divide them into subsets. We have the old-fashioned kind where a stranger forces himself on a woman. We have statutory rape where an adult male (over eighteen in most states) has carnal knowledge of an underage girl. We have date rape where the boyfriend doesn't understand the word "no" and forces himself on his date. Marital rape is another category. Here, a married or estranged husband forces himself on an unwilling wife.

Does anyone really believe that we would have the number and types of rape occurring today if men respected women? Surely, the arousal triggered by the images on our TV and movie screens has contributed to the aggressiveness these men use. If their heroes are seen beating up on women and those women seem to love it, is it any wonder they would seek to accomplish the same reaction? Incest is skyrocketing out of control. I can't find any disagreement among those who hold themselves out as experts on this subject. Stepfathers, brothers, stepbrothers, uncles, fathers and grandfathers are preying on our children because there's no one saying they shouldn't. The kids are taught to dress sexy from an early age, and the adults (mostly men) have run out of other fantasies.

We next have those young women who have become a part of the sex industry. The world has always had its young prostitutes, but today we have young girls by the tens of thousands posing for pictures, trading their bodies for drugs, and dancing nude on stages from coast to coast.

But you don't have to go to the seedy side of town to see teen-agers exploited. Turn on the TV, go to a theater, or rent a video. See teen-age actresses (and younger) play the part of sex partner, prostitute, or victim of incest. See them pose in sexy attire or assume sexy poses to advertise a new make-up line or hair product. Is it any wonder that they end up playing many of these roles in their real life? Meanwhile, they serve as the role models for other teen-agers.

How can anyone read about the tragedies that have been listed above and continue to believe that the sexual revolution has benefited the girls and women of our culture? Have the ladies benefited from the availability of sexually exploitative literature, steamy soaps, or erotic movies? What has been the price of the stimulation this material provides? By virtue of continuous propaganda that open and free sex is romantic and generally without consequence, our women are much more likely to experiment with sexual activities outside of marriage. They are far more likely to be promiscuous. As a result, they are far more likely to fall prey to all of the above consequences. In addition, the reality of their own romantic and sexual experience with their husbands or boyfriends can never compete with the carefully posed and rehearsed images on the screen. Therefore, their personal love lives are diminished by comparison. This can greatly affect the strength of their relationships as they continue to expect what their partner can't hope to deliver. As the husband fails repeatedly to provide the kind of sensitivity, passion, and creativity in the bedroom that their wives see on the screen, many of these wives come to believe they can only find this kind of romance with another partner. The result is infidelity and divorce. Otherwise excellent husbands are turned out because they are not living up to false images of what it takes to be a good husband and lover.

Sexual liberation has another negative consequence for the women. Because all the men they knew prior to marriage couldn't be trusted to be faithful, the new bride finds it impossible to trust her new husband to remain faithful in the marriage. This is made doubly difficult in that she probably knows about his sexual experience prior to their marriage. This lack of trust has drawbacks too obvious to list here.

One undisputed fact about the nature of women is their desire for security. This security is most specifically sought in the marriage relationship. Almost all women would like to have a lifetime partner with whom they can share bed, board, children, and economic strength. Along with the sexual revolution came the end of the concept of lifetime commitment. In fact, it would be easy to suggest that for many, it meant the end of any type of commitment. Marriage has become a relationship of convenience. If either partner decides for any reason they would like to end the marriage, there are virtually no legal barriers and very little social stigma for doing so; commonly, divorce proves to be an economic benefit for the man. As a result, the woman is once again the victim. She is the one left to care for the children while holding down a full-time job. She is the one who ends up with a dramatically lowered standard of living. According to the Bureau of the Census, the spouse with custody of the children sees income drop by 37 percent within four months of separation.

Even if she is the one who wants the divorce, it is usually as a result of one or more of the marital problems stemming from the sexual revolution as outlined above. He is unfaithful. He does not respect her. She believes the man she is seeing outside the marriage will marry her after the divorce. She believes that another man will be more romantic. She doesn't trust him, even though she has no actual knowledge of untrustworthy behavior. She doesn't feel secure and believes she will be more secure in a new relationship.

Stop and think about it. These problems, to the extent that they existed at all prior to 1966 and the sexual revolution, were minor problems that only happened in somebody else's family. Today, there is only the rare individual who has not been devastated by one or more of these at the most personal level. It is hard to see how any woman could believe that women as a group have benefited from so-called sexual liberation. However, isn't it true that men have a really good deal, now that what was once so "expensive" is now, so cheap?

Surely, the answer is contained in the question. It is the rare individual who, having a choice, prefers the cheap. We may settle for cheap if we can't afford quality, but given the resources, most of us will take a Jaguar over a Ford Fiesta. To most men, the idea of marrying a woman who has not given herself to another man is still an exciting idea. Most emotionally mature men understand that a woman who has the discipline and integrity to maintain her virginity until marriage is exactly the kind of person who will likely have the discipline and integrity to stay true to him after marriage. Almost any man will have a happier marriage if his wife has a strong sense of self-worth. She is far more likely to feel good about herself if she has been successful in maintaining her standards and has not felt as though she was just a sex object.

Let's next consider the proposition that men have gained because they now have such access to sexually erotic material. One would suspect that the average man would, if asked, be pleased that he can look at pictures of erotically posed women. Most who take advantage of such material would likely, if asked, expect to be disappointed were they to be deprived of such opportunities. Dig a little deeper, however, and you will likely discover the following: (1) most feel viewing such material is wrong; (2) almost all have tried to stop and felt compelled, like an addict, to continue their involvement with pornographic material; (3) most who use these materials have sexual dysfunction in their marriage; (4) many find more pleasure in masturbating while using the pornographic material as stimulation, than they do in making love with their wife. Possibly the most important negative associated with this material, however, is the well-known and documented tendency for serious addiction. As with many addictive behaviors, the individual is satisfied, at first, with mildly erotic material. Many boys get started with underwear commercials or the pictures in a school text on human sexuality. These soon lose their allure, and more erotic fare is sought. For many, the journey doesn't even stop with *Playboy* or R-rated movies. The next step may be to hard-core or even sexually violent magazines or videos. Like the alcoholic, drug addict, or gambler, the last rush is never enough. The need for kinkier and kinkier material grows until it begins to dominate the victim's life. At some point along the way, looking at pictures just doesn't cut it anymore. For many who are addicted to pornography, the next step is an insatiable desire to act out the scenes that are most exciting. In many cases this results in rape, brutal beatings, mutilation, torture, and even death to the hapless women who come into contact with such an addict. It is unlikely that we will ever know how many in our society are addicted in varying degrees to pornography. Most men would probably rather admit to beating their wives than to needing porn in their life. My personal suspicion is that a very large percentage of the men in Western culture are troubled by their desires for this material.

In what other ways are men the losers in this dream age of open sex? Surely, there are very few men in even these liberated times who are happy if their wife has an affair. Studies show that men are more emotionally devastated by divorce than are women. It would seem to me that almost every father would prefer that his daughter maintain her virginity until marriage. I suspect that very few men are overjoyed when their daughters or wives watch naked men on the screen or go to a male strip joint.

Then there's disease. In the section on the negatives for women, I suggested that sexually transmitted diseases (STDs) are a bigger problem for women than for men. By no means should this suggest that men aren't being harmed by these treacherous diseases. We all believe that men are tough, and this can imply insensitivity. Most would agree that there are lots of men who are not in touch with their feelings. This results in a mistaken belief that men who love and leave their women feel no remorse, guilt, or other damaging emotions.

Society also thinks that men who run away as fast as they can from their pregnant girlfriends, or who pay for the abortion, continue their lives without emotional consequences. Based on personal observation of friends and acquaintances over the years, I offer, however, that this is a myth of the highest order. Men may seem to be unfeeling on these issues. I would propose that they are just better at covering up their emotions. Men have gotten what they wanted, and it has turned out to be a bitter prize: (1) free sex means cheap women; (2) sexual liberation for their girlfriends extends to their wives and daughters; (3) pornography becomes a secret addiction and a potential source of danger to their loved ones; and (4) STDs create fear instead of excitement in new relationships. Alas, our men finally ask themselves, "What kind of a man would stoop to these things?"

If women, men, and teen-age girls are all among the losers in the revolution, maybe it's our children who have benefited. It is still commonly believed today that openness about sexuality will result in our kids being more honest and less repressed about that aspect of their lives. It was thought that the baby boomers who led the revolution would be quick to answer all their children's questions openly and honestly. In return the kids would seek their answers at home instead of from their peers.

Unfortunately, none of these expected benefits developed. Today's parents are no more likely to be open and honest with their kids about sexuality than their parents were. Today's youth don't turn to their peers as often as the boomers did, since they can learn all about sex from their schools, movies, television, and pornographic magazines. And what is the wholesome method being unanimously espoused by these sources of information: "Do what you want. There is no right or wrong. The more sex you get the better. The more partners you have, the better you are as a person." Are our kids less repressed?

One can only come to a conclusion about that question by seriously considering the definition. Which is more liberating? (1) being under pressure to discipline oneself, or being under pressure to follow the crowd; (2) being under pressure to follow a set of moral standards, or being under pressure to break away from all standards; (3) being under pressure to think of things to say and do with a new girlfriend or boyfriend, or being under pressure to perform sexually for that new relationship; (4) being under pressure to resist the temptation to participate in behaviors likely to disrupt or even destroy your life, or being under pressure to pull the trigger in a game of Russian roulette.

Amazingly, it seems as if most preteens are more enlightened about all this than many of the so-called experts. Most ten and eleven-year-olds I come in contact with today are no different than those I grew up with. They are not very interested in sexual issues, and they very commonly stick their tongues out and groan, "*iiiikkkkkk*" when they see a TV couple merely kissing. Why do our cultural leaders insist on pushing our kids into this arena before they wish to go there? To sell more movies, records, or magazines?

If profit motive is the answer, why haven't the consumer groups come to the rescue of our kids in the way that they have with regard to smoking? There is an uproar over cartoon characters as cigarette spokes-creatures but no equivalent concern about the cartoon girlfriend of Roger Rabbit. We have major campaigns by the media to discourage our kids from smoking, drinking, or taking drugs, but the very same people fight against telling our kids to abstain from sex. So where does this leave the children of this sexually liberated generation? Dying from suicide; dying from AIDS; running away from home; failing in school; joining gangs in search of a "family"; taking drugs and drinking; becoming the victims of incest and child molestation—and all of these at record levels. Our kids are the innocents in all of this. Women are big losers in this new age. Men, the apparent winners, are losers as well. Our kids, who aren't able to protect themselves against this scourge, are dying, emotionally and physically. And then there are the pre-born, the true innocents, being aborted by the millions. How can a society that places so much value in the life of a spotted owl, a tufted titmouse, or a laboratory rat turn around and kill over a million human babies every year? How can a society that passes laws to protect migratory geese, elephant tusks, dolphins, and whales also pass laws helping people to kill their own offspring merely because they still reside in the womb? How can a society that spends so much time and money on the attainment of emotional health allow children who are not yet considered old enough to vote, smoke cigarettes, or have their ears pierced without parental consent make the decision to take the life of their own child without parental advice or adult counsel?

There has to be a winner in this revolution, doesn't there? There must be some group who has profited financially, emotionally, or spiritually to such a great extent that we as a culture are willing to allow the victims and losers to continue to suffer in order that the winners will not lose their spoils. But who is left to be a winner? (1) advertisers who believe that sexy ads sell their products or that sexy and politically correct TV and radio programs attract viewers who will see their ads; (2) movie and television-related businesses that believe that they will attract large audiences and critical acclaim because of their product's sexual content; (3) publishing companies who expect to profit from sexually provocative material in magazines, newspapers and books; (4) producers of outright porn; (5) those who are sexually deviant or who desire to participate in practices that most feel are unacceptable in civilized society!

The question of winners and losers seemed most clear in a conversation I had with an associate shortly after Madonna's book, titled *SEX*, was published. He was quick to defend the book and its content. I wondered aloud whether such a book would cause young people who admired Madonna and saw the abhorrent behavior pictured in that book to be more inclined to experiment in bestiality, pedophilia, or homosexuality? He responded that he wasn't sure, but he wouldn't mind driving down the street and finding a nude Madonna hitchhiking by the side of the road. I replied that I understood how he might like seeing Madonna that way. However, I asked, would he want his own daughter hitchhiking nude? His very soft reply was, "No. I guess not."

Let me use this forum as I will many others in the coming months to ask these questions of all those who have made money by using women or girls as sex objects, portrayed homosexuality as a perfectly acceptable lifestyle alternative, or promoted promiscuity and/or abortion among our young: (1) Would you want your fifteen-year-old daughter or granddaughter to be actively involved in sexual intercourse, oral sex, or anal sex with one or more boys at this time? (2) Would you want your fourteen-year-old son or grandson to be engaging in sexual activities with adult male homosexuals? Your daughter with a lesbian? (3) Do you hope that your children and grandchildren will participate in group sex, violent sex, sadism, masochism, sex with children or animals, public nudity or sex, or extramarital sex? (4) Are you anxious that your daughter be provided the experience of having one or more abortions, children out of wedlock, or give up a child for adoption? (5) Are you just waiting for the day when one of your children comes home and tells you that they have HIV or one of the other virulent STDs that are ravaging our population? No matter what you may think about the morality of those who are profiting financially or artistically from the sexual revolution, I suspect that almost everyone would answer all of the above with a resounding NO! My final questions to them would be: In that case, why in the world would you put your audience at even a small additional risk of having to endure one of these maladies in order that you might gain an extra dollar of income or one positive review of your artistic effort? How can you justify even one of my children dying at the hands of one who has been inspired by a violent sexual episode that you wrote, directed, produced, or screened? Why would you desire one thing for your own family, but be willing to sacrifice the emotional, financial, or physical well-being of my family in the interest of artistic freedom?

Now, let me ask you, the reader, an important question: Assuming any of the sellers of sex actually profit from the sexual revolution and pass the acid test above, but still feel somehow led to continue to spread unhealthy and immoral ideas, should we as a society trade our emotional and physical health, the welfare of our children, or our very nobility as a people for the profits of these groups? The time has come for *action*! The time has come to hold those who would destroy our children's lives in the name of profits to be held accountable for their actions. We have closed down entire industries in the past to save the lives of a few children who might otherwise hurt themselves on a toy or in a game. How can we tolerate an entertainment and publishing industry that would injure or kill all of our children and many of our adults?

In a later chapter I will call on all Americans to send an unmistakable message to the media. There is only one message they seem to understand. They truly believe that you and I vote with our channel changer and our ticket purchases. The time to change your vote has arrived. *We must take action!*

Four

Predictable Consequences of the Continuation of the Sexual Revolution

❖

The ACLU regrets to inform you of our opposition to SB 2394 concerning sex education in public schools. It is our position that teaching that monogamous, heterosexual intercourse within marriage is a traditional American value is an unconstitutional establishment of a religious doctrine in public schools. . . . We believe SB 2394 violates the First Amendment.

Letter to California State Assembly Education Committee, reprinted in its entirety in *Children at Risk* by Dr. James Dobson and Gary L. Bauer

Our world is full of Chicken Littles, yelling that the sky is falling. There are many individuals and groups which have much to gain or lose from predictions of calamity on the horizon. Even the well-meaning among us are quick to spot the slightest trend and turn it into a coming crisis of cataclysmic proportions. Twenty years ago we were warned of a coming ice age because the amount of carbon dioxide in our air caused by the burning of fossil fuels would cool the earth. Today we are told that our use of hydrofluoric carbons is destroying the ozone layer and that fossil fuels are creating a greenhouse effect. Result? Global warming, which will surely end life on earth as we know it. One can speculate that in another twenty years we will be talking again of ice age.

Possibly this will be due to the reduction in use of carbon products.

I don't wish to be counted among those who cry out before there is a crisis. Some did try to rally the troops to the cause of turning back the sexual revolution earlier. There were those in the early sixties who believed our society was on the way to a repeat of the decadence associated with the fall of Rome. We were reminded of the excesses of the Roman emperors with their orgies, pedophilia, and human sacrifices. These early prophets of doom were scoffed at for their beliefs. Many who saw the sexual revolution as a needed swing of the pendulum away from puritanism, laughed at those who criticized the trends toward public nudity, explicit sexual behavior in films, and more freedom of sexual expression between unmarried partners. For most, these early experiments in "openness" seemed worthy of a try—at worst, they were seen as the frivolous expression of youthful rebellion. Almost no one imagined the potential consequences that lay ahead.

Those who expected the worst were relieved to see an end to the blatant group sex and other outrageous behavior of the seventies. It seemed as if the pendulum was set to begin its unrelenting swing back to historical standards of conduct. Unfortunately, that has not been the case. That step forward was met with many new steps backward. The last decade has seen our brave new world descend ever deeper into a pit of moral relativism. The most despicable behaviors, activities which would never have been spoken about in polite conversation, are now the subject of television sitcoms and Supreme Court nomination testimony.

It is now too late to cry out that the sky is falling. For those who have died from suicide, AIDS, and other sexually related diseases, the warning is of no use. For others whose lives have been disrupted, hopelessly injured, or completely destroyed, the time for action was yesterday. The crisis is already here, and undoubtedly your life has already been touched by it. Maybe not directly, but almost certainly a close relative or friend has had their life turned upside-down by some aspect of today's sexual practices. I have had friends and children of friends who have died of AIDS. I have had close associates, friends and even relatives who have suffered from unwanted pregnancies, STDs, and other emotional and physical diseases as a result of promiscuous behavior. The crisis is already here, but there is so much more to come. You may have a hard time imagining that our civilized Western society could ever consider the ideas that follow, but in 1960, it would have been unimaginable to hand out free condoms to fourteen-year-old girls at school, paid for by tax dollars. In 1970 there would not have been a single school in the country which could have even sold condoms in dispensers in the bathrooms. In fact, many states still prohibit their sale in public rest rooms today. Here are a few things our future holds if we stand on the sidelines and fail to turn back the tide of immorality which is creating new standards for our entire society with each passing day.

The Total Destruction of the Family

The family will actually become the relic on the ash heap of civilization that many already claim it has become. Fortunately, the traditional family is far from meeting its end as of 1993. The conclusions cited by those who would like us to believe that the traditional family is already dead are misinterpretations of statistics at best, and downright misstatements for the most part. Those who are in favor of continuing the disastrous experiment in human sexuality and relationships believe that they can prove the premise that virtually no one still lives the life of the ideal "Leave It to Beaver" family. If they can succeed in convincing us that it just isn't fashionable, or possible, or necessary to strive for that ideal, it will make it much easier for them to press forward with legislation that empowers and enriches those who are living in "alternative" relationships at the expense of those who are living in traditional families. To date they have been extraordinarily successful. They have convinced the public that less than 10 percent of the population lives in a traditional family. Those who support this proposition have been the benefactors of tax changes which have dramatically increased the tax burden of families. They have lobbied for and successfully enacted laws which have changed the very definition of "family" to include anyone who rooms with another person of whatever sex, for whatever reason.

Let's take a closer look at the statistics used as a basis for the demise of the family. You may be reminded of the kinds of statistical "games" played by Kinsey in the early days of the sexual revolution. In order to get the absurdly low number of less than 10 percent, you must use the narrowest definition of "traditional family" possible. The definition used by leading anti-family spokesperson, Congresswoman Pat Schroeder, is "a working father and stay-at-home wife with two children living at home." On the face of it, this seems like an excellent definition of the traditional family. However, the use of this narrow description means that the following families having a working husband and/or stay-at-home wife would not be considered traditional: (1) a man and woman living as husband and wife with one child, or three, four, five, six, or more (any number but two isn't traditional); (2) a man and woman living as husband and wife who have decided against or who are unable to bear children; (3) a man and woman living as husband and wife whose children are now grown and living on their own; (4) a widow or widower living with any number of children; (5) a family in which the wife works. In looking back at history, all of these would seem to fit the model of traditional family.

Additionally, while the majority of those polled feel that it is best for a woman to stay at home as long as she can during the child-rearing years, it would be far from correct to suggest that traditional families have not included women who provided income to the family. In both farming and industrial cultures, the wives of those in the middle and lower classes have always been very active in providing income. (For example, many took in wash, sewing or ironing. Others grew fresh fruit and vegetables in the garden and traded with neighbors or took it to market. Still others worked as cottage laborers.)

A more appropriate definition of traditional family might be: persons related by blood, heterosexual marriage, or adoption. This definition would exclude two or more unrelated persons of the *same* sex living together, whether or not they are sexual partners. It would also exclude two or more unrelated persons of *opposite* sex living together, whether or not they are sexual partners.

Why am I haggling over these definitions? Why not in-clude homosexuals and singles? Why can't unmarried couples or even roommates be included? Because society has a stake in the traditional family. In fact, many of our leaders have loudly proclaimed the importance of the family in the stabil-ity of our culture. And who would stand up today and argue that the disintegration of the family has benefited Western civilization? No one can look at the conditions of our inner cities and believe that illegitimacy and divorce have been a blessing to the poor.

Support traditional families as the ideal, and institute the laws that make it easy to marry and hard to divorce, finan-cially beneficial to have and raise children in a stable family unit, and fashionable to be responsible for those to whom you have committed yourself. Then stand back and watch a new revolution take place. Watch as stable emotional and economic family units produce children who are emotionally stable. Notice boys and girls shun gangs as substitute families because they have a loving home. Visualize a time when a teen-age girl will find all the love she needs from her father and not feel compelled to go looking for it from any young man who promises it. If the anti-family group can convince us that the family is dead (in much the same way that Kinsey et al. convinced us that 10 percent of the population was homosexual, and that everybody was sleeping with every-body else), we will undoubtedly continue moving toward that end. Divorce will become easier and easier, and mar-riage will be little more than an excuse for a party. The language "till death do us part" will be replaced by "till we don't love each other any more." If we continue down the slippery slope, our future will include children raised by the state almost from birth. Young men will have absolutely no reason to marry or feel responsible for children they sire. Young women will decide this isn't equitable and will merely abandon their children to the state. This may seem far-fetched, but it isn't. Right this minute, unmarried inner city teen-age girls are deliberately getting pregnant because "it's the thing to do." (Nothing is far-fetched!) Homosexual couples will raise children acquired from sex with a person hired for that purpose. Or they will use adoption, artificial insemination, or scientific technology's amazing trick. But the future is already here. In many states it is already legal for homosexuals to do any or all of the above.

In other words, in the society of the future, there will be no such thing as a family unit where adults are committed to each other for a lifetime, or to the raising and nurturing of children for their lifetimes. Those who are still doing so will be in the small minority and will be viewed as strange. Of course, without such commitment and structure, individuals will be taught the value systems of whoever is in authority or whoever is having sway over popular opinion at the time, whether this be a Ghandi, a Hitler, a Lincoln, or a Saddam Hussein. Without the structure of a family with its built-in characteristic of unconditional love, adults and children alike will seek to find their identity through temporary peer relationships, authority figures, and the media. Shared values will be impossible, the concept of social contract all but forgotten. Chaos or totalitarianism are the only possible choices. Freedom and democracy couldn't possibly survive in such a society.

Sexually Transmitted Diseases at Plague Proportions

Millions will die from STDs. Man was designed to be monogamous. To the extent that the human species defies its biological prerogative, it will become diseased. The sexual act creates a wonderful environment for disease, and the illicit acts associated with homosexuality, pedophilia, and bestiality provide an even better seedbed for the spread of germs. Even those who don't believe that God is using disease to punish people who would ignore his commands with regard to conduct and sexuality can't help but conclude that those who are promiscuous will very likely see negative impacts on their health. (This, however, is not to detract from the likelihood that God is sending very definite signals to stay away from the stove or risk getting burned.)

While it may seem preposterous to propose that there will be new, yet unknown diseases like AIDS, there are new sexually transmitted diseases appearing every year. In addition, we are seeing new strains of gonorrhea that are resistant to penicillin. The current approach to conquering STDs rests on spending ever larger amounts of money on cures (even though we already spend more on AIDS research per person infected than any other disease) and encouraging the use of condoms. However, after years of education in the latter, a recently released study indicated that only 20 percent of sexually active (unmarried) women between the ages of fifteen and forty-five use condoms. Of those, only 20 percent used a condom during their last sexual encounter. In other words, less than 20 percent of women in this statistical grouping are insisting on condom use with any regularity. To make matters worse, condoms are known to be less than 75 percent effective, due to actual failure of the product, improper use, or failure to follow through on good intentions to use them. Some say that it is unrealistic to expect our youth to abstain from sex (although we certainly expect them to abstain from murder, thievery, drug use, and even rudeness). I would propose that it is unrealistic to expect condoms to prevent pregnancy or disease. Instead, leaders believe that those they govern are incapable of exercising the discipline necessary to abstain from sexual involvement outside of marriage. Thus, the abstinence message is offered, if at all, as an aside. Unless we can find a way to change the message we are sending to those at risk, many will become very ill, large numbers chronically ill, and many more will die.

Sexually Explicit Materials in Sex Education Classes

Our children will receive ever more modern sex education classes. It can't be that far away from a time when live action videos with human subjects will be used to show proper condom installation and use. Surely, you say, this couldn't happen. Today, some junior-high students are instructed in the use of condoms using cucumbers. If I had suggested that this might happen three years ago, you would have said, "Surely this couldn't happen."

I would further predict that classroom films will also show the proper method for petting, oral sex, anal sex, homosexual encounters, and sex with animals. Don't believe it? The University of Oregon has already produced a video entitled *SAFE* to instruct special education students in grades seven through twelve in the proper techniques for using a condom. This video uses a nude male who puts the condom on, moves behind a screen to ejaculate, and then reappears to show the removal process. This video is in use now! There are schools today that describe all the above acts in writing for grade-school kids. Wouldn't the instruction be much more meaningful in full color? (I ask facetiously). It would be much more likely to hold the students' attention!

It would seem likely that our first- and second-graders will soon be discussing their own sexual preferences. It seems likely that schools will offer play-acting opportunities for our grammar-schoolers to provide them with politically correct ways of seeing homosexuals. I'm sure you still think I'm off my rocker. Right now—today—first-grade teachers are instructed in some school districts to include references to homosexual "families" as an option in any discussion held about families. A major battle took place in the New York City schools between school district administrators, teachers, and others fighting to introduce such a curriculum. Who were their adversaries? Parents. Amazingly, in order for day care providers to get their license in the state of Washington, they must provide instructional material for and discuss "all family configurations."

Today, our preteens are still taught not to allow anyone to touch them in certain ways or on certain parts of their body. This is likely to be reversed. In the future these children will be taught that as long as such touching is done in a loving and tender way, it is all right. Preposterous, right? I dare you to tell me that in 1965, a sex education class curriculum could have even been discussed which would have suggested "outercourse" for junior-high students as an appropriate sexual expression and a birth control method. Any such teacher, principal, or board member would have been run out of town on a rail. But your own school district may be offering outercourse instruction at this very moment.

There are academicians, educators, and organizations that are very seriously calling for the acceptance of pedophilia (adult sex with children) as a lifestyle choice and proposing that adult/child sexual contact can be beneficial to both. Now! Not in the future—now!

Pornographic Materials Available in Libraries

Pornographic materials depicting every type of depravity will be available at your local library without restriction to your children. They will be able to view and read about the types of sexual acts that would probably make you blush if they were mentioned in mixed company. This material will undoubtedly also be in video form. I can hear many of you laughing out loud at such a prospect. Too late. It is already happening right this minute. *SEX* (Madonna's book) offers depictions of homosexuality, pedophilia, bestiality, various masturbation poses, and nude hitchhiking scenes. It is already available in public libraries. In the face of parental concern about this book, librarians are yelling "censorship." Some would have us remove copies of Mark Twain's works because of the historically common slang word, "nigger." As unfortunate as it is that this word creates a not-surprising uneasiness in the hearts of black Americans, it is just too ironic that we would be asked to censor classics because of such sensitivity, but retain works of questionable value whose potential for serious harm is obvious. Even as *SEX* is at your library now, I suggest that more vulgar output awaits. You see, the ground has been broken. Now those who would desensitize our children to sexual vulgarity are waiting to press on with more explicit fare.

Explicit Sex Acts between Same Sex, Adults and Children, Humans and Animals, and More at the Movies

Coming soon to a theater near you will be explicit homosexual sex acts. Homosexual kissing has already started, and to be sure, more is to come. We will also be treated to children being sexually and erotically seduced by parents, uncles, or neighbors. Seven- and eight-year-old girls will be depicted enjoying their seduction. Young boys will be seen in intimate relationships with men. By now you must suspect that I wouldn't make such a statement without being able to back it up. We, as taxpayers, have already paid an artist to create photographs of a young girl seated in such a way that you, as the viewer, can look up her skirt. We have already paid to have photos taken of schoolboys in homoerotic settings. The National Endowment for the Arts called this material "art." I call it illegal exploitation of minor children for money.

Therefore, if some call it art, surely our movie theaters will dare to cross the line and show the work of filmmakers who express themselves in this new art form. Then it will be time to see incest. Oh, that's right, we've already seen incest in Stephen King's *Sleepwalkers*. Then it must be time to explore violent anal rape of children of both sexes by adult sexual offenders. Nope, old hat. We were already offended last year in the movie *The Prince of Tides*. Without its hazy, dreamlike sequence depicting these crimes, the media could not have assured the further softening in the public attitude toward incest and its subsequent acceptance of it as an alternative lifestyle. Now we have Academy Award-winning movies which offer the most decadent examples of human depravity imaginable. I'll just give you one example you may or may not be aware of. This movie told us the story of a man who kidnapped and imprisoned his female victims. He then tortured, killed, and skinned them. That's right, skinned them! His purpose? He was a transsexual. He wanted to create a perfect female body suit, so he could wear it when he wanted to be a woman. Can it get worse than that? I can't imagine anything more horrible. Remember, however, this film was not an illegal production that had to be sold in the black market. It wasn't something only shown at your local porn theater. It wasn't even rated X. The movie, *Silence of the Lambs*, won several major Academy Awards.

Why am I worried about the future of America? Because a scant thirty-five years ago it was not possible to show the slightest nudity on the screen. Where will we be in another thirty-five years? Where will we be next year?

Television—Anything and Everything

It's easy to predict what will be coming on TV. You will eventually see anything and everything in prime time that you can now only see in a porn movie house. Does this seem extreme? Consider your shock and outrage when only a handful of years ago the first "d——" was uttered on network TV. How far we have come in such a short time. Now it seems that almost every show must include two nude, single adults in bed together discussing how wonderful "it" was. Los Angeles Channel 13 (KCOP) recently showed *The Killing Fields* at 10:00 A.M. during Christmas vacation along with its many uses of the "f" word. A viewer contacted the station about their questionable decision to air the movie at that time, and received a response from John Shahauer, who had no problem with the program or the air time.

Today, we would be shocked if a fifteen-year-old female character, faced with a decision about having sex with her boyfriend, would waste much time on the abstinence arguments, much less decide against a night of sexual expression. We have already seen virtual nudity on network TV. Surely we are only weeks away from our first test of full female nudity. Once the stations have satisfied themselves with that, they will push the bounds to show the youngest-looking, unclothed eighteen-year-old girl the purveyors of this trash can find. Then comes the inevitable slip-up where a fifteen-year-old who lied about her age is seen in nude scenes.

What could I be talking about? You see, this is the same path taken first by the men's magazines, then porn movies, followed by regular release films and videos. Television is just taking the same path a few years later. However, what it took the magazines twenty years to achieve, the movies accomplished in ten, and TV will do in five.

Human Lovemaking Replaced by Animalistic Sex

As we move toward the year 2000, the sex "act" will have become just that for a large percentage of the population. These unfortunates will have never participated in a sexual union that has grown out of mutual respect and love, coupled with a lifelong commitment to share each other exclusively. This hedonistic approach to sex in which the parties are only after the momentary orgasm and touch of another human being will not result in fulfillment. Then, as

with any lust, comes the search for the greater and greater
high, when those who would follow this path will seek out
ever more erotic opportunities, all, of necessity, ever more
illicit and dangerous. For some there will be the thrill of
taking sex by force or with violence. For others there will be
the thrill of the idea of being raped or taken sexually with
violence. For still others there will be experiments with children, same-sex partners, groups, animals, human waste,
bondage, sado-masochism, torture, mutilation, and even
murder.

The future? No! It's already happening. You say you
don't know anybody who engages in any of these things? Let
me ask you: In 1965 did you know any woman who had slept
with ten men and was proud of it? Did you know of any men
who lived openly as homosexual lovers? Had you ever seen
a major movie star totally naked in an erotic sex act? Did you
know anybody who had ever died from an STD? Did you
even know an unmarried couple living together? The future
is already here in large measure, and it is already too horrible to imagine when we read about it all at once. We have
become so used to this vile material as a part of our daily life
that the consequence of its impression upon us and our
children is not in the forefront of our thinking. We have
become desensitized.

To see how we can be slowly seduced into thinking all of
this is somehow normal, consider the effects of hot water on
your skin. If you turn the water on as hot as it will go and
expose your hand to it, you will yank it back in pain. However, if you start with warm water and slowly increase the
temperature, you may be able to endure even the hottest
temperature. You may still be scalded, but your skin has
been slowly prepared or desensitized to the heat.

As a culture, we have been slowly prepared. What can it
hurt to show pictures of a girl in her negligee? So what if you
can see the faint outline of the breast underneath? Surely
there is nothing wrong with the negligee pulled down reveal-
ingly. Other cultures have shown the full breast without
embarrassment. You get the message. Just keep pushing the
edge of acceptability further and further. The purveyors of
sexually erotic material have led us down the path over and

over again; this is familiar territory for them. We are now
very close to the end of the road.

Anarchy

Our sexual decadence will surely be matched by our
immorality in every other part of our lives. If we are left
without respect for one another regarding our most personal selves, how can we have any respect for mere possessions, freedoms, beliefs, or feelings? We are well on our way
to losing all respect for our leaders. Are we about to enter
an age of anarchy? In many cities we are already there. We
can't even keep our teens from devaluing property (with
graffiti) or from thievery—concepts in which they should
have been well schooled by kindergarten.

We must act now. Many have voiced these words for
other causes, but I sincerely believe that there has never
been a more urgent need for results: We must act before it
is too late, and we are at the eleventh hour. I have presented
very specific proposals for working toward changes for our
own lives in chapters 5 through 9. In chapters 10 through 13
you will find a complete strategy for changing our neighbor-
hoods, our schools, our cities, our nation, and the dangerous
message being offered by the various media. What I propose
is not easy or inexpensive. It requires commitment, courage,
time, and sacrifice. But then, this is true of any war worth
fighting. And it is a war—the war for our hearts, souls, and
spirits, and those of our children!

Five

An Urgent Appeal to Teen-age Girls

❖

Eighty-nine percent of girls reported having been the subject of sexual comments, gestures, and looks. Eighty-three percent said that they had been touched, pinched, or grabbed. The survey included girls ranging primarily from 10 to 18 years of age.

Santa Monica Outlook,
24 March 1993

Would you take a drink from a glass you found sitting by the side of the road? Would you eat food you found in a stranger's trash can? Would you take a drug that would give you two or three minutes of intense pleasure, but would have a very good chance of causing a burning itch on a part of your body for the rest of your life?

Do you need a boyfriend so badly that you would be willing to ruin your life in order to have his affection for a few weeks or months? Do you enjoy sex so much that you'd be willing to risk death or disease in order to do it just one more time? Is sex and having a boyfriend such a big deal that killing your unborn child is just a necessary though annoying side effect to avoid being inconvenienced?

It is my great hope that this book will be read by every teen-age girl in America. Someone needs to tell you the truth. You are the big losers in the sexual revolution. You are the ones suffering from infections caused by sexually transmitted diseases. In some areas of the country the infection rate is one girl out of two or even higher. You are the ones getting pregnant and having to make a life and death decision for your baby.

You are the one who will be in the clinic with your feet in the stirrups when they kill your unborn child.

You will be the one who hands over your beautiful newborn child, the symbol of what you believed was love, to another couple, never to be seen by you again.

You will be the one who, after deciding to keep your baby, will live in poverty, never having a chance to complete your education, and who will spend your teen years changing diapers instead of attending proms.

None of these things are likely to happen to your boyfriend (what was his name, again?). No, he's off doing this to some other girl right now. He's finished his education. He's got a good job. He drives a nice car. Maybe he even married a virgin and has a nice little family now.

You need to stand up for your rights today. You need to tell the world you are a valuable human being, not a sex machine. You may want to be loved by a man, but you want that man to love you for a lifetime, not for one night or for a few months.

If you don't take this stand, you are very likely to contract an STD during your sexually active teen years. If you allow strange boys to engage in sexual intercourse or oral sex with you, your chances of getting sick are much higher than eating out of a trash can or drinking from a glass found by the side of the road.

As a teen-ager, you may have a tendency to believe that you are immune to major disease or death. A few of your friends may die in car accidents or of drug overdoses during your teen years, but you aren't going to be the one. And when it comes to STDs, you don't know anyone who has one of those. Right? Wrong! Nobody brags about having genital warts or herpes. Chlamydia, HPV, and gonorrhea aren't usually the favorite subject for lunch chatter. So how many of your friends have an STD? Start counting the people around you. Every time you get to six, one of those is already infected. Every time you get to twenty, one of those will become infected with an STD this year. One in six. Seems like a pretty high number, right? Let's subtract all the people who have never had sex (like children), or who have only had sex with one uninfected partner. They can't get the disease, and they represent two in three Americans at least. So, if you have sex with more than one person and are not certain whether or not any of them have an STD, your odds of becoming infected increases to one out of two. It is so hard to imagine that premarital sex is worth the risk. Heads, you win—tails, you lose! Fifty-fifty. If you win, you get a few minutes of pleasure (maybe). If you lose, you are risking your health, your ability to bear children, your reproductive organs, or your life. Seems like a very bad bet!

You might question next just how serious such diseases are. Except for AIDS and herpes, they can be cured, right? So there might be a little itching or pain. Why all the fuss about STDs (except AIDS, of course)? Itching and pain—sometimes severe and recurring—are possible symptoms. Add to the list disfiguring sores and warts on your genitals. How about urinary infections, arthritis, tubal pregnancies, miscarriage, increased likelihood of contracting other STDs including AIDS, infertility, cancer, and death?

That's enough, I suspect, but it isn't all. You can give it to your baby. You can pass it on to other sexual partners. Both of these can happen even though you may have never had a symptom. You can carry the disease without knowing you have it. So can your boyfriend. He may tell you he is clean, and he won't know he isn't giving you the whole truth. He won't know he just gave you a serious disease with major potential for harm.

There are ten major STDs and three less important ones. There are also numerous diseases that can be passed by sexual contact. The following describes the thirteen that are generally passed to you by an infected partner during sex. (Warning: The material in this section is not easy reading. You may want to skip ahead and not face the reality. I encourage you to risk losing your appetite now rather than risk losing your own life or your ability to bear children later.)

Chlamydia

Chlamydia is an infection which has afflicted over four million people in the United States alone. It is particularly rampant among adolescents and young adults; as many as 25 percent of this age group are estimated to be affected. The percentage of those who have the disease among the sexually active may be 40 percent or higher.

Chlamydia is often silent. As many as 75 percent of women will not be aware they have contracted it until complications begin. Moreover, it is possible to be infected over and over. Each time your chances for serious consequences increase by 25 percent. For instance, there is a 25 percent chance that if you are infected once, you will damage your reproductive system enough to experience chronic pain, tubal pregnancies (a major cause of maternal death), or infertility. If you contract it a second time, you now have a 50 percent chance of suffering these complications. A third time and you have a 75 percent likelihood. After four infections, there is an almost 100 percent certainty that the reproductive organs are so badly damaged that the woman will not be able to conceive.

Other possible consequences of this epidemic disease include abscesses that may result in removal of the uterus, tubes, and ovaries; infections of the liver; and death. A mother with chlamydia may pass it on to her child at birth. This may result in an eye infection, middle ear infection, or even pneumonia. It may also result in a premature birth.

The good news is that for 25 percent of those who have this disease, the symptoms will be experienced immediately. These "good news" symptoms include burning with urination, urethral discharge, pain in the lower abdomen, or fever. These symptoms can be cured with medication. The only remaining inconvenience is the 25 percent possibility of minor to severe damage to the reproductive system.

The bad news is that 75 percent of those who have chlamydia won't know it until they have more advanced complications or have passed it on to others. Finally, if a woman is infected with chlamydia, she has an increased chance of becoming infected with another STD. When chlamydia infection is combined with the destructive ability of other simultaneous infections, the dangers of more advanced complications increase.

With four million sexually active adults affected by this infection each year, it would seem to be enough by itself to cause intelligent young women to abstain from sexual activity until married. I hope the above description is giving young female readers something to think about. Unfortunately, this is only the first of over twenty-five possible STDs that you might be rewarded with the next time your boyfriend asks you to "prove your love."

Gonorrhea (the "clap")

Also known as the "clap," gonorrhea was once considered one of those STDs "under control." However, with 1.4 million new cases in the U.S. each year, it is very much out of control today. There is almost a 40 percent chance of contracting gonorrhea from an infected partner after just one sexual contact.

Here is a quick list of possible short-term and long-term symptoms and consequences of infection with gonorrhea: burning or pain with urination; pus-like discharge from the urethra; frequent urination; inability to urinate (requiring catherization); swollen or cystic Bartholin's glands (requiring surgery); vaginal discharge; pelvic inflammatory disease (PID); infertility; eye infection in babies; arthritis; chronic pelvic pain; complete hysterectomy; painful intercourse; tubal pregnancies; and abscesses of the vulva. Like chlamydia, gonorrhea is very often carried without symptoms, either partner passing it along without knowledge. It may also mean that it reaches advanced stages before there are symptoms.

Genital Warts (HPV)

I am forever indebted to obstetrician/gynecologist Dr. Joe McIlhaney, Jr. for his help in preparing this chapter. I will admit to borrowing freely from his book, *Sexuality and Sexually Transmitted Diseases,* as well as from materials provided by the United Way and the Department of Health and Human Services for this portion of the book.

First a quote from *Sexuality and Sexually Transmitted Diseases:* "I have seen women delay seeing a doctor until warts as large as a fist were hanging from their vulva." A brochure

produced by the American Social Health Organization, a
United Way Agency, describes genital warts as "growths or
bumps that appear on the vulva, in or around the vagina or
anus, on the cervix. . . . They may be raised or flat, single or
multiple, small or large. Some cluster together forming a
cauliflower-like shape."

Would it matter to you if this disease had no other
symptom? Wouldn't such a disfigurement be something you'd
want to avoid at all costs? Incredibly, at least 750,000 people
per year are infected. Recent studies have shown that as
many as 33 percent of women have the human papilloma
virus (HPV), which causes these warts.

I would like to report that an ugly wart on your private
parts is the only result of this disease. Unhappily, 8,000
women *die* each year from cancers of the vulva, vagina, and
cervix associated with this virus. This is far more than currently die each year from AIDS. Like so many STDs, HPV is
sneaky. Sometimes the warts are so small or hidden that you
don't see them or recognize that they are warts. Thus they
have time to become cancerous without the victim ever
knowing it.

Once again there is great potential harm to babies born
to mothers who are infected. They may develop warts in
their throats. Surgery is required to remove these warts, and
there can be permanent scarring of the vocal cords.

Genital Herpes

Do you ever get a cold sore on your lip or around your
nose? Maybe you've never suffered this way, but you surely
know someone who does. Not a pretty sight and pretty
uncomfortable, too. Imagine for a moment having one of
those sores in or on your sex organs. Imagine the discomfort
of having one on the vulva, inside your vagina, on the cervix
area, or around your anus. Typical symptoms include pain,
burning, itching, or tingling.

Herpes, like the common cold, has no cure. Unlike the
common cold, you have it for life, and you don't have to
"catch" new germs to have a new outbreak. You may or may
not have recurring symptoms. Some women have outbreaks
several times per month. Intercourse, surgery, illness, tight

clothing, fatigue, diet, menstruation, skin irritation such as sunburn, or even stress can bring it on. Some men and women who are infected never have any symptoms (starting to sound familiar?). They can spread it to their sexual partners, however. You can also pass it on to your baby during childbirth. The risk of passing it to a baby is low, but the death rate of those babies who are infected is 65 percent.

What are the real chances that you'll get herpes? Thirty million Americans have it now, and there are 500,000 new cases per year. Every time you have sex with a new partner you dramatically increase your odds of getting any one of these diseases. Let me add a final note on herpes. According to the American Social Health Association, the presence of herpes sores in the genital area increases the risk of contracting the AIDS virus.

Syphilis

Consider this myth:

Nobody gets syphilis any more, certainly not in a country as advanced as the U.S. Besides, if you get it, all you need is a shot of penicillin. This myth needs to be exploded. First, plenty of people are becoming infected with syphilis. One hundred thirty thousand adults contract the disease each year, and over forty thousand infants are born to mothers who have the disease. After increasing dramatically in the late eighties, the percentage of adults contracting syphilis declined slightly in 1991. Unfortunately, the number of babies born with syphilis continues to rise at a frightening rate.

The cure for syphilis is a shot of penicillin. And if you're allergic to penicillin, there are alternative drugs available. The problem is that about 50 percent of those who catch syphilis either don't show any symptoms, disregard the symptoms they do have, or are misdiagnosed by their doctors. As a result, 50 percent of 130,000 people each year don't know they have this disease until it is past its early, most easily treatable stages. Among these are the mothers who then unwittingly infect their newborns or encounter other negative consequences during pregnancy. Those who have the disease can pass it on, whether or not they are aware they are infected. Over 50 percent of those who have sex one time with an infected partner will get syphilis.

In the first stage, a canker sore may appear on the vulva, in the vagina, inside the mouth, or on the lips. There may be several sores. Later, this sore will generally become a hard knot. During the second stage, several weeks or months later, there may be symptoms such as fever, headache, fatigue, skin rash, and enlarged lymph nodes. Grayish, moist growths in the mouth, under the arms, and beneath the breasts may appear and become open sores.

If left untreated, syphilis will next move into a latent period for months or even years or decades. However, when it returns, it does so with devastating effects including: problems in the blood vessels, deterioration of the central nervous system, damage to bones, peripheral nerves, liver cells, and heart valves. Babies can catch syphilis while still in the womb, resulting in any number of horrible consequences: 38 percent of infected pregnant women experience spontaneous miscarriage, stillborns, or the death of the baby shortly after birth; 41 percent of the babies have bone problems, liver or spleen defects, or damage to eyes, ears, or nose.

AIDS (HIV)

You would have to be living in a cave in the middle of Antarctica to be unaware of the symptoms and consequences of AIDS. Beyond the massive controversy about AIDS, one thing about which few disagree is that those who catch the HIV virus will all develop AIDS eventually, and that there is currently no cure for AIDS.

The early stages of the disease have their own set of symptoms—weight loss, fever, diarrhea, shingles, and commonly enlarged lymph nodes. These will seem like minor irritants compared to what is to come. *AIDS* stands for Acquired Immune Deficiency Syndrome, which means that the body has a reduced ability to fight off other diseases.

Different patients develop different manifestations of the syndrome and succumb to a variety of diseases, but they are all deadly. Some of the most common are pneumonia, cancer, and encephalitis. The afflicted waste away as their body is assaulted with one or more of these infections and numerous others as well.

Sharon Nichols, whose brother recently died of AIDS,

puts it this way: "The mental and physical torture of this totally debilitating disease is almost beyond description. Victims and their families can only watch in horror as their bodies often become terribly disfigured and weak."

Like so many STDs, your partner may be HIV positive and not know it. Incredibly, the government doesn't require reporting of this disease to health authorities, so someone who is HIV positive and knows it has no compulsion to tell their sex partners, past or future, about it. There are now many cases of infected persons pursuing very active sex lives and (sometimes deliberately) passing the disease to many partners.

You have undoubtedly heard that AIDS is primarily contractible by homosexuals and drug users. It is true that in the U.S. the disease has thus far been more prevalent in those communities. However, as of 1988, 10 percent of all AIDS cases were women. This was up from only 3 percent in 1981. Women are four times more likely to contract AIDS from a man than a man is to contract it from a woman. Amazingly, in the only study of its kind, thirteen out of seventeen individuals who had unprotected sex with an infected partner contracted the disease. Two out of twelve who used a condom also became infected.

HIV is highly contagious, so it should not be surprising that 30 percent of the babies born to mothers who are HIV positive are themselves infected with the AIDS virus.

How do you contract AIDS? It can only be transmitted through an exchange of infected bodily fluids. At this time only blood and semen are known to have the necessary concentrations to pass the HIV virus. Homosexual, heterosexual, vaginal, oral, and anal sex are all highly likely modes of transmission. Needle-sharing by drug users, blood transfusions, and other situations in which infected blood or semen comes in contact with open sores are extremely risky.

Hepatitis B

Hepatitis B is transmitted in almost exactly the same way as AIDS: through semen and blood. It is not as contagious as AIDS and only causes severe illness in 10 percent of those who contract it. However it is possible for hepatitis B to lead to cirrhosis or cancer of the liver. Either of these can result in death.

You can have it and not know it. In fact, 90 percent of those who have hepatitis B will have no symptoms and can easily pass it on to their sexual partners, dentist, doctors, or others who come in contact with their bodily fluids. It can also be passed on to a newborn. More than half the babies who catch hepatitis in this way develop liver problems, including cancer.

Vaginitis

You won't die from vaginitis. You won't even be that sick. But you will have a vaginal discharge which will likely be quite smelly. You will have some severe itching of the vulva. You are likely to have burning of the vulva and pain with intercourse. There are two types of vaginitis which are commonly transmitted sexually. The most unpleasant is trichomonas vaginalis. Approximately 3 million women are infected each year. The other form is bacterial vaginosis, which is present in 10 to 20 percent of sexually active women of reproductive age.

Pubic Lice (crabs)

Pubic lice are little bugs, that cause itching and are embarrassing. Think about this as well. If you acquire crabs from your boyfriend, it's pretty likely that he has other STDs as well.

Scabies, Molluscum, Contagiosum, Chancroid, Granuloma Inguinal (GI), and Lymphogranuloma Vernereum (LGV)

These STDs are either of minor consequence to your health (like crabs), or they are very rare. For more information on all of these STDs, I heartily recommend you read *Sexuality and Sexually Transmitted Diseases* by Joe S. McIlhaney, Jr., M.D.

There are many in our culture today who can't accept the idea that God would have purposely created these diseases to discourage sin. It would seem to me in reviewing the nature and seriousness of these horrible scourges that any other explanation would be far from adequate. Each and every one of these epidemics could be ended in short order if people were content to stay with one sexual partner for life. Instead, most of them are at epidemic or pandemic proportions due to promiscuous sexual behavior.

You have a choice: have sex with many boys or men, in and outside of marriage, or make love with one man to whom you are married. This is totally your choice! The consequences of your decision may be the difference between life and death, disease and health, beauty and blemish, fertility and barrenness, the life or death of your children. And these consequences are only those associated with STDs.

Boys

I'd like to take this opportunity to talk to you about boys. Whether you are twelve or nineteen, or even the mother of a teen-ager, there are certain things about boys (and men) that you ought to know. In some cases, you may already sense the things I am about to tell you. However, most young women, and many older ones, seem by the way they act to be unaware of what makes men do the things they do. Hopefully, you will talk about what you read here with your parents, girlfriends, and others you trust for advice. They may be able to add to and confirm the truthfulness of these comments. It is my hope that this information will help you achieve healthier, happier relationships with the boys in your life, as well as with your future husband.

Boys Are Visual

One of the most interesting differences between boys and girls is what excites them sexually. It is not unusual for a boy to be stimulated by the mere sight of an underwear advertisement in the paper. Almost any young man will be excited by a picture of a girl or woman in the nude. This may seem odd to you, girls, since you don't react the same way to pictures of men. You may be curious about how men look in the nude but probably wouldn't go out of your way to see such a picture.

You've also noticed men watch the way a woman walks, or practically drool over a girl with lots of cleavage. Many women think that this natural tendency on the part of boys is disgusting or immoral. However, it is really just a part of man's normal personality. In the comments to teen-age boys in another section, I suggest that they should keep this leering under control. It is bad manners and leads to other negative consequences.

It is no secret that men like to look at women. Unfortunately, many girls use this knowledge in an effort to attract young men, commonly inviting big problems. When you see a boy who is attracted to your body, especially if this attraction arises from an erotic interest, it is because he has seen a lot of "skin." This generally results in a relationship based on seeing your body. His interest in you is limited to seeing more and more. Rarely does he ever get to know the rest of you. And once he's seen everything of yours his natural desire is to want to see something new, somebody new. His desire to see another girl's body has nothing to do with how pretty your body is. He just wants to see something different.

When a boy is attracted to you because of your personality, intelligence, or charm, then he is more likely to want to learn more about those aspects of you, elements that grow and change and really have no end. Does this mean he isn't interested in seeing those parts of your body that are normally covered up? Not if he's normal. However, he will be far more patient about satisfying his need to "see" if his interest in you is based on who you are, rather than what you look like.

Action

Many of the following suggestions may be things you've been told by your mother or teacher. However, now that you know why these are important, I hope you will take them to heart.

1. When seated in a dress or skirt, always keep your knees together or your legs crossed. When you cross your legs, do so carefully and discreetly.

2. Check your necklines in the mirror to insure that when you bend over, you aren't putting on a show.

3. When you try on a bathing suit, check all aspects for modesty. Young men will be particularly interested in seeing any part of the curve of your breast: top, side, or bottom. They will also be quite appreciative of seeing any part of

your derriere (rear end). Even exposing the little roll of flesh at the top of your thigh can cause a lot of staring. It goes without saying that a low-cut front on the bottom of a two-piece, or showing any pubic hair, will result in plenty of interest (of the wrong kind).

4. Almost all boys are even more excited by what they can almost see than what they can actually see. This is known as a "tease." I have seen young girls wrapped in a towel after a shower come into a room with male friends present. That towel might cover every part of her private anatomy. However, the knowledge that she is nude underneath can cause a young man's hormones to race almost as fast as if she came out totally nude. Thus, when the girls took off their bras in the seventies as a show of freedom, it turned out to be another kind of show. When you wear an outfit without underwear in order to eliminate lines, the male imagination has a field day. If you go slipless and pass in front of a well-lit door, all eyes will be on you, or at least on one part of you. Tight-fitting clothes that reveal details of what's underneath have the same effect.

Some of you are starting to protest. You are worried that if you don't appeal to the visual interests of a man, you will be at a disadvantage in your quest to find a date or a mate. If you keep all your secrets under wraps, you'll be seen as a prude, and all the other girls will get the "good" men. May I propose that the opposite is true? Girls who flash their anatomy may get a few more dates. They may even get one or two dates with some of the "good" men. When it really counts, however, these will be the young women who will be used, abused, and discarded. They will have the least success in their marriages. They will pay the price throughout their lives by believing that they are not worth anything if they aren't showing skin.

Men Are Stimulated by Touching

The same curiosity in men that causes them to want to "see" whatever is covered up also causes them to want to explore by touching those parts that are generally off limits. This is where we get the saying, "Men have Roman hands and Russian fingers." As you are getting to know your boyfriend, he is very likely trying to see how far he can go in this business of touching. It begins with holding hands, putting his arm around you, kissing, putting his hand on your leg, or rubbing your arms or back. Of course, you like all of this, too. You like it partly because you like the touching, but for you there is also the romance and the excitement. However, as with looking, the more the young man gets to touch, the more he wants to touch. He is never satisfied with what he has already done. He wants to explore something new. And as discussed above with "seeing," once he has touched everything you have, he will want to touch somebody else.

Action

1. Make it clear early in every new relationship that you don't agree with any type of petting. Holding hands and walking arm in arm or with arms around the waist or shoulder is fine. His hands don't belong on your leg, the exposed skin on any part of your body other than your hands or face, or any part of the front of your body, whether clothed or not.

2. Most boys will try to touch you by slowly progressing from safe areas to new, forbidden territory. As most aren't very talkative in these situations, they won't ask permission. They'll just see how far they can get before you object. Gently remove his hand to the old safe spot. If he persists, gently tell him that you aren't interested in going any further than you already have. You may want to reassure him that you like him, but that his future with you will be short if he persists in his efforts.

3. You may have already progressed to some petting with your current boyfriend. If you want the relationship to continue, stop at your current level and immediately reverse the process, allowing him less and less touching on each subsequent date. You will want to explain to him that your change of heart has nothing to do with your feelings for him, but you aren't ready for lovemaking, and that continuing with the petting will surely lead to both of you wanting more until ultimately only sexual intercourse will satisfy both of your appetites.

4. Commonly, the boy will have one or more arguments

for continuing his pursuit of forbidden fruit. He may suggest that everybody does it, or that you are a real prude if you don't. He may get mad or pout if you don't give him his way. He may back off a little, say sweet nothings in your ear, and then try, try again. Most men can be very persuasive and clever in their attempt to get what they want from you sexually. Moreover, the older or more experienced they are, the better at this game they are likely to be.

Once again, you have excellent responses available to you for each action he takes. I don't mean to imply that these are easy, only that they work if you'll use them. If he says, "Everyone is doing it," tell him you doubt this is true. But even if it were true, you are your own woman and don't wish to follow the crowd.

If he gets mad and pouts, let him sulk. You may want to explain that your decision has nothing to do with your interest in him, but that you are looking for a man who is more interested in your mind than your anatomy.

If he tries the technique of sweet talk to overcome your previous "no, thank you," merely repeat your statement, remove his hand again, but this time more sternly. The third time, you may want to call an end to physical contact for the time being, and suggest that you both need to cool off and discuss the future of the relationship while sitting about three feet apart.

Boys Love the Chase

Always keep in mind that male humans are excited, first and foremost, by the challenge of winning your love. The number one mistake made by women and men in the past thirty years has been messing with the mating game. Boys want to catch you, although there is an old saying that suggests "the boy chases the girl until she catches him." There is very little fun for the guy if the girl pursues him. He may be flattered, and he may respond by starting a relationship. However, for the most part, a man will feel less manly if the girl is obviously (rather than subtly) running the show. In fact, as the romance progresses, he will start to feel smothered and trapped if you call him, write him notes (except in response to his), or are always hanging on him.

There can be no doubt that we are living in times where this concept of men doing all the asking can try a girl's patience. With so many young women doing the asking, there is a fear that all the good ones will be taken by these more aggressive girls. I can't implore you strongly enough on this subject. *Hold out.* Wait for a boy who has enough confidence in himself to ask for what he wants. It will be worth it.

Action

1. Don't ever call a potential or current boyfriend unless it is absolutely necessary. If he calls and you are unavailable, give directions that he call you back at a certain time; don't call him back.

2. Don't ask men or boys out on dates. Even when the relationship is quite far advanced, use hints to get your steady to ask you out. Let him think he is in control, even if he's not.

3. Only rarely initiate affection. For the most part, let him take your hand or arm. Let him offer a kiss. Just as men were born with a built-in desire to lead in these areas, women know how to send signals that they are ready to have their hand held or to accept a kiss.

4. Make him work for your interest. He really wants to open doors for you, help you with your coat, and protect you from any kind of harm. He will love you more for letting him do these things. (If he doesn't feel this way, you don't want him anyway.)

If you don't give him the opportunity to (or, in fact, insist) that he do these things, he will stop. However, you will both lose as a result. He wants to be your knight in shining armor, and you want him to be romantic. If you won't let him do these little things, it is very unlikely that he will do things like send flowers or love letters.

Boys Have a Very Strong Sexual Drive

Most women will never understand the amount of interest young men have in sexual matters. Scientists maintain that this has much to do with a hormone that boys have in abundance, called testosterone. It is this hormone that causes the man's voice to deepen, his face to grow hair, and his personality to be more aggressive than the average woman in most areas.

When a boy enters adolescence, he soon finds himself unable to completely control certain aspects of his sexuality. In many cases, long before he really wants to have anything to do with girls, he becomes preoccupied with studying his female classmates' changing anatomies. As a result of such interest, or sometimes for no reason at all, he finds himself becoming excited. Unless he is in a position to "walk it off," there is really very little that can be done except grin and bear it.

If these minor situations can cause a boy to get sexually excited, imagine what happens with the first kiss, or the first time he puts his hands on a girl's bare knee. Once a boy has an erection, the natural desire of the body is to relieve it.

I don't bring this up to make you feel sorry for him, or for you to let him use this as an excuse for you to give in. You see, a boy in this state isn't in love; he thinks he's in dire need of relief. If it doesn't come, he'll get over it, and there won't be any lasting damage. However, if you give in, the damage can be devastating and permanent.

On the other hand, I think it is valuable for you to understand why your boyfriend will use so many approaches, games, arguments, or even physical strength to persuade you to take care of his sexual needs. It is equally important to understand that once he is satisfied, unless he is totally committed to you in marriage, you become a sexual object. Worse yet, you are a used sexual object. The bloom is off the rose, and he will now begin looking for a new flower.

This fact of life does not mean that all men are "jerks." That same sexual desire in boys is mirrored in your life in the form of the need for security and intimacy from someone who will love you unconditionally. And many a young lady foolishly trades away her virginity, her self-esteem, and sometimes her health or even her life in a futile attempt to keep one of these jerks around. This same jerk might have become a wonderful lifetime companion if our heroine had kept her clothes on.

Action

1. Treasure your body and your virginity as the prize for the boy or man who honors and respects you enough to court you without sexual activity. There is so much to learn about each other through talking, studying, or enjoying leisure time together.

2. When you date, go in groups. Eliminate opportunities to be alone and unsupervised. Agree together that this is what you both want in order to reduce opportunities for sexual exploration.

3. Make a commitment to yourself, your parents, and to God that you will maintain your virginity until marriage, and determine now never to even consider an extramarital sexual encounter of any kind once you are married.

4. Be prepared to deal with the following: "If you love me, you'll have sex with me." Notice I used the expression "have sex" rather than "make love." In a committed, loving relationship, the sex act is the ultimate expression of the love two people feel for each other. In a premarital or extramarital situation, the sex act is primarily for the physical satisfaction of the male and meets some physical and emotional needs for the female. However, it is not "making love." In fact, if you pay attention to the words of your boyfriend, your friends, the actors on TV and in the movies, and even yourself, you will notice that the expression for sex outside of marriage may vary from the tame but unromantic, "sleeping together" to various vulgarities. Your words will give you away. Your easy response to the statement "If you loved me, you'd sleep with me," is "If you love me, you'll respect my decision to save myself for you until our wedding night," or simply, "If you love me, you'll wait."

5. Recognize that this won't be the last argument that your boyfriend will offer. He will also suggest that it's a good idea for couples to "try on the shoe before you buy it." You may wish to respond that you resent his comparing you to a shoe. Shoes don't get pregnant, catch venereal diseases, or feel bad when their boyfriend never calls again. Additionally, if you fail to buy a shoe you try on, the next potential purchaser doesn't mind at all that someone else has already

put on the shoe—but that may not be the case with people. Finally, point out that he isn't buying you.

6. He may point to the writings of well-known sexologists who propose that sexual experience prior to marriage will make for better sex in the marriage. You could respond that every survey on the subject shows that marriages of those who maintain their virginity until marriage have a substantially higher chance of success than those who have wide experience prior to marriage. Listed below is a short list of the advantages of abstaining from intercourse until marriage.

1. Your husband will be extremely pleased. It will be a plus in his eyes for your entire marriage.

2. You are much more likely to end up with a "good" husband, as those who aren't so "good" will move on when you won't "give in."

3. You will enjoy a much higher opinion of yourself.

4. You will not have to sneak around and lie to parents and future boyfriends about your experiences.

5. While some of your friends will never admit it, you will gain their respect for your stance.

6. You will not become pregnant out of wedlock.

7. You are much less likely ever to have an abortion.

8. You will greatly enhance your chances of completing your educational and career goals.

9. You will greatly diminish your chances of ever catching a sexually transmitted disease. (The chance will be zero if you marry someone who is also a virgin.)

10. You will be much healthier emotionally.

11. You will be an excellent witness to others who might follow your example.

12. You will dramatically increase the likelihood of having healthy children when you do become pregnant.

13. You will be much more likely to survive to adulthood.

14. Your discipline in this area is likely to benefit you in every other aspect of your life. You will be less likely to smoke, drink, take drugs, overeat, or indulge yourself in other harmful ways.

15. You will improve every aspect of your health as a result of not using various birth control devices.

16. You will substantially reduce your chances of becoming a single mother with all the hardships to yourself and your child that come with that status.

17. You will be far less likely to ever experience the pain of waking up to an empty bed.

18. You will never have to deal with the guilt that goes with premarital sex, sneaking around, lying to future boyfriends, having an abortion, becoming infected with an STD, or giving up a child for adoption.

19. You will never have to deal with yourself on the question of the morality of your action.

20. You are far less likely to ever be raped.

21. You are far less likely to be in a position in which you will be sexually assaulted in any way, including being sexually harassed. When you are clear in your mind and heart about your sexuality, most men can clearly read the signals and will not go where they aren't wanted.

22. By not having even one premarital sexual partner, you will clearly never be in a position to be promiscuous. Many girls believe that their first partner will be their only one. Unless he's your new husband, that is very unlikely.

23. If you never engage in premarital sex you are much less likely to ever engage in extramarital sex.

24. You will please yourself.

25. You will please your parents.

26. You will please God.

Avoiding Sexual Temptation

If you desire to maintain your chastity until you are married (and if you do, I commend you for making one of the wisest decisions you will make in your entire life), you are going to be faced with hundreds of prickly thorns to be avoided, thorns which could destroy your flower before you find the man you want to marry. Only thirty years ago, the situation was totally reversed. Any boy or man who was intent on deflowering a young lady was faced with getting past the thorns. Today, virginity is seen as a kind of bondage to a system where men have all the fun while the women stay pure and miss out.

In 1962, schools divided girls and boys when they took sex education, allowing both groups to be more open, less shy about the subject, and making the subject more respectable. Birth control was never discussed, and abstinence until marriage was the only rule. Homosexuality and other sexual deviancies were not discussed. Today, sex education is taught in a co-educational setting, which results in less openness on the part of the inexperienced students, and provides a platform for brazen, experienced students to titillate the class with stories of exploits; sex becomes less romantic and more common. Condom use and application is frequently described in detail as are other methods of birth control, and every abnormal sexual behavior is considered a lifestyle choice—the latter sometimes also described in detail. The entire experiment assuredly results in the feeling that sex is an unfeeling act of pleasure derived purely from our animal instincts.

Less than thirty years ago, the movie industry would not expose a woman's breast. Television would not show a married couple in the same bed together. Off-color language in mainstream media was confined to a few minor words in the movies. Though films, records, and even TV sometimes dealt with imprudent sexual behavior and various characters were obviously stepping across the moral boundaries, for the most part, they ended up paying for their misadventures. Lack of responsibility had a natural consequence and lack of character was never glamorized.

Only one generation later (actually, the turning point occurred between 1966 and 1969), every form of entertainment is a billboard for unlicensed sex and perversion. In the 1992 presidential race, we were even told that "character doesn't matter," and a large part of the population heard that message and said, "Hooray, if it doesn't matter for the president, surely I have even more license than ever."

When your mother was very young and went out on a date (if she is over forty-five), she usually didn't have to worry whether the young man would try to make a move, put the pressure on, or even rape her. Her concern was whether or not he would try to kiss her on the doorstep when he walked her there after the date. A recent poll of young teen-agers indicated that half of them believed that today's Romeo deserved a sexual reward if he bought his date dinner. One third said he even had the right to rape her!

How can this be a better system for you as a young woman? Why should you be under so much pressure to risk your emotional and physical health, your future, and even your life? Why do those who hold liberal values about sex believe that you are better off in this environment? Lovemaking used to be seen as tender and romantic. Now sex is seen as animalistic and just one of many sensual pleasures available to those who hope to find happiness in personal pleasure.

Action

1. Make a decision today to maintain your virginity until marriage. Find a way to express this commitment to your parents and/or your best friend. Also make the commitment to God. Let your Heavenly Father know your desire for purity, and ask His help in maintaining it.

2. If you have already lost your virginity, make a pledge to take on secondary virginity. Stop now, and make the pledge to parents, friends, and God that you will wait until marriage to express your love for another man through sexual intimacy.

3. Ask your parents to have you excused from any sex education class that is co-ed, that encourages any type of birth control other than abstinence, or that promotes homosexuality or other sexually deviant behavior as merely a lifestyle choice. You don't need to have those in authority challenging your decision to maintain a healthy and moral lifestyle.

4. You'll notice that each of these first three involve your parents. Several major studies have shown that the best way for you to reach adulthood sexually pure, drug- and alcohol-free, and with a good education is to have a good relationship with your parents. In every such relationship with another human being, it takes two to make it work. You can't control whether your mom or dad will work toward having a loving, caring relationship with you. However, you can control how you act toward them.

5. You won't find similar advice through any popular media outlet. You won't even easily find the results of several major surveys on the subject. Yet, just announced at the time of this writing are three studies all coming to the same conclusion: The most important factor in human health and happiness is a strong personal religious faith.

Look around you. Who is least likely to get divorced? Who are least likely to get STDs or AIDS? Which groups have the lowest suicide rate? Which have the most successful parent/child relationships? Which are most successful in their careers or have the best grades? Which are the class leaders, and those most likely to help those in need? Yep! They're the ones who have a deep, abiding faith in a personal God.

How can you become a part of that group? Become friends with someone who you know has such faith. Attend church (try several before you find one that best fills your needs). Ask your parents or a trusted friend to help you in your search. If you already have such a faith but still find yourself engaged in improper sexual activities, see your pastor today. If he doesn't help, look for a counselor who shares your faith. (School counselors are likely to tell you to do what you want. They won't have to live through the consequences.)

6. Avoid television, movies, records, and other media that deal with sexual topics or that show intimate sexual acts. Don't believe that you are immune from the stimulation. These types of materials are just as addictive as alcohol or drugs. Also avoid those shows that promote illicit sex as acceptable. Advertisers spend a few minutes of each hour convincing you to buy their products, and this use of their money is very effective in causing you to change your opinion or form a new one. Imagine how much more effective a two-hour movie might be at trying to convince you that premarital sex is wonderful, or that everyone should try homosexual behavior at least once.

7. Wear a symbol of your decision. When I got married and started to wear a wedding band, there was an immediate change in the way women talked and acted around me. They

knew I was now off limits—taken. You can accomplish the same thing by wearing a piece of "key" jewelry. It can become the symbol of a young person who prizes his or her virginity. Sometimes described as the "key to your heart" or the "key to your virginity," a ring, necklace, bracelet, or other key-bearing ornament tells your date exactly where you stand. It goes a long way toward discouraging an otherwise aggressive boyfriend.

8. Select your friends wisely. If you are hanging out with a crowd that thinks differently than you, find a different group. You are not likely to change your current friends' minds on this or any subject, although you may want to lend them this book as a start. On the other hand, it is very hard to ignore the constant pressure of friends who want you to join them in their sin. It is always difficult to be the pure one in any group, no matter how strong you may think you are. It is uncomfortable for those who are doing what they know is wrong, and it is uncomfortable for you because you want to speak out or help them.

Some Good News and Some Bad News

First the bad news. I know a very attractive young woman who matches her beauty with brains and personality. However, don't take my word for it. She is senior class president of a large urban school, was nominated to be homecoming queen, and was selected as prom queen. She is also a straight A student. No one asked her to the prom. Her values are well known and would differ little from those espoused in these pages.

If you take the abstinence pledge and make the decision to wait for a boy who will "ask you out" and treat you with respect, you may not have as many dates as some other girls. You may question your own looks, personality, and appeal. The wait will be worth it, though there will be times you will wonder. The mature young man who agrees with your position on these issues is the kind of person who you can count on to make a lifetime commitment and raise your children with tenderness.

Any time you wonder which type of man you would prefer to marry, refer back to the story of my wife, Pam. Her low self-esteem sent her into the arms of any man who gave her a moment's notice. When the moment was over, she was left more lonely than before.

There is a man for every one of you. Wait for the right one. In order to have an even better understanding of the strange creatures called men, be sure to read the next chapter on teen-age boys. My daughter said she gained a lot from that reading. You can help to encourage more young men to adopt the values outlined in these pages. The way to do that is contained in chapters 11 through 13. I hope you will join in the sexual counter-revolution proposed there.

SIX

A Man-to-Man Talk with Teen-age Boys

❖

I once thought I'd tell my young son that anything goes–so long as he used condoms. Now I'm not so sure. Not only do I want my son to live, I don't want him to miss out on longing–longing for what he isn't yet ready to have.

Ellen Hopkins, "Sex Is for Adults,"
contributing editor for *Rolling Stone*,
quoted in *Citizen Magazine*,
19 April 1993.

Maybe I'm living in a fantasy world. After all, I'm forty-five. That makes me an old man to you, and it may be that you would question whether or not I can relate to what's going on in your world today. Even so, I'm going to take a chance that what I'm about to say to you will make perfect sense.

I hope and believe that you would not like to be responsible for any of the following:

1. causing someone to die;
2. infecting someone with a horrible disease;
3. ruining someone's life;
4. having one of your children grow up in desperate poverty;
5. purposely hurting someone who is smaller and weaker than you;
6. destroying your own future;

7. keeping a family from having children;
8. hurting your mom and dad;
9. embarrassing your friends and family;
10. interfering with your relationship with God.

Some who read the above list probably wouldn't feel all that bad if they did these things. Those who feel that way won't get much out of the material that follows. Most of you thought to yourself, "Not me. I would never be involved in any of those things. If I were, I would feel terrible guilt and shame." I have some very bad news for you: It is very likely that you already have done—or soon will do—something that will result in one or more of those harms. Statistically, you are a high risk to have premarital sex with someone. If you do, chances are very, very high that you will be a party to one or more of the above results.

When I was your age (back in the Stone Age), boys who could find a girl that would let them "do it" only really worried about getting her pregnant. Oh sure, his folks would be mad if they knew, and it was recognized as a sin; but the main worry was having to marry this girl and raise the kid.

This is called a "double standard." Boys were supposed to get "it" if they could. Girls who "did it" were tramps. I am well aware that times have changed. Today, lots of girls do it, and they aren't necessarily looked down on. In fact, sometimes it's the virgins who are laughed at, right? But another thing that has changed is the consequences. Sure, she might get pregnant, but there's so much more.

Let's see. She might get an abortion. Now you're off the hook, right? But . . . maybe you don't want her to abort *your* child. Or maybe she won't want you in her life anymore after she has an abortion. Now who gets hurt? Maybe you both think an abortion is a great idea . . . today. However we're seeing that years later some men and many, many women feel really bad about having taken that life. And some women are injured during the abortion and are now infertile.

Perhaps she might decide to keep the baby. Let's examine your options. You could marry her. Whoops, she doesn't want to marry you. But maybe she wants you to pay the baby's expenses for the next eighteen years. The government's getting really clever about making sure that happens too.

Now, or maybe sometime later, you might want to see your baby, or your young child, or your teen-age boy. Maybe she and her new husband don't really want you around that much—or ever. They might even move out of the area. Maybe you never have any other kids, and your little girl wants her stepdad to march her down the aisle, not you.

Here is a fairy tale ending. You do get married. You drop out of school and get a job at a fast food restaurant. You and your new wife live in a great little apartment and drive a beat-up old car to work and the store. Chances are over 50 percent that you'll get divorced. Oh! The odds are even higher that your child and its mother will end up living in poverty.

Let's forget about pregnancy for a while. Could it be that this wasn't the only girl you ever had sex with? Were you her first? Did any of her previous friends have AIDS? Maybe you're carrying some other disease from a previous relationship. Will you be giving her a case of genital herpes so she can be in pain once a month for years into the future? Maybe you gave her chlamydia. She could end up sterile or get cancer and die. Here's a good one. You give her the new treatment-resistant strain of syphilis, and she gets pregnant, and the baby gets it, and . . . *isn't sex wonderful?*

It can be wonderful. If you've had sex with a girlfriend, I'm sure you already know how nice the physical sensation is. But there is no way to explain to you how incredible it is to "make love" (which is different than "having sex") with someone whom you truly love. How do you know you are really in love? A good clue is that you care enough to be willing to make a lifetime commitment to your lover that you will share one another exclusively.

Of course, if you're bringing a lot of problems from previous relationships into that marriage—for instance, many previous sexual partners; earlier children or abortions; or maybe a sexually transmitted disease (STD)—it could reduce your enjoyment of this potentially wonderful love relationship. By now you may be thinking that getting sex from a girl may have some pretty horrible consequences. I've really only touched on a few of the worst results. If you read the rest of this book, you'll get to see a few hundred more.

I might be over the hill, but I do understand that containing your desire isn't always an easy thing to do. There is plenty of pressure from lots of places pushing you toward "getting some." All I can promise is that if you'll read the next ten pages or so, and really think hard about what I'm going to say, you will have a much better hope of enjoying an active, normal, healthy, and immensely satisfying sex life.

The Physical Pressure

You are walking down the hall at school when all of a sudden . . . Wow! Evelyn Smith, also known as "the Chest," bends over right in front of you just as you accidentally looked that way (well, not exactly accidentally, but anyway). You got to see everything! Uh-oh. Your body is reacting to the sight. How are you going to prevent classmates from noticing? That's pressure.

There may be a bunch of things about women that we as men will never understand, but one thing they can't hope to know about us is the feeling of an erection that won't go down. As a teen-ager that condition can be happening many times per day. That's pressure. To make matters a bunch worse, any kind of sexual situation brings it on. The slightest kiss or even less—can make it happen. But if things go beyond that kiss at all, the pressure, it seems, could kill you. *That's pressure.*

All that pressure is very normal. God built us that way in order to insure that we would want to make babies. After all, not all men are that interested in babies, but almost all of us are interested in making them. Unfortunately, that pressure also gets us into trouble. It is because of that pressure that we men are prone to use every trick in the book to get girls to have sex with us.

The question for you today is not whether you are man enough to convince some young lady to let you do it, but whether you are man enough to control your urge until you get married. Maturity is in large part defined by our ability to control our urges.

Make a Decision

First, decide that something is important enough to you that you will do everything in your power to accomplish

what you set out to do. Most of the time, these decisions
come all at once. You just make up your mind that you want
to abstain and decide that you want to avoid the negatives
associated with premarital sex and enjoy the benefits of
lovemaking only within a committed marital relationship.
Sometimes the decision happens over time. You may be
persuaded by some of the things you read here and have
your mind opened to the idea. Then later you may hear
another argument that makes sense. You may even find
yourself changing friends to those who agree with abstinence, and they can influence your thinking. It could also
happen that a particular experience could be the final ingredient that brings you to a decision to stay pure.

Best of all would be coming to know Jesus as your Lord
and Savior. By doing so, your relationship with God and the
study of His Word would move your heart to accept abstinence as not just one possible solution, but the only possible
solution for you. Does that mean that you wouldn't ever slip
and fall? Not at all. Christ's followers are still tempted into
sin. However, it would mean that you would be far less likely
to be promiscuous or to have even one sexual relationship
outside of marriage. It would also mean that you would be
able to seek divine forgiveness and quickly move again to
stop such activity.

Stay Out of Harm's Way

In other words, you want to avoid those situations which
increase the likelihood that you indulge a bad habit. Things
are no different when it comes to sex. Here are a few things
you want to avoid:

1. pornographic books, magazines, movies, videos,
   music, etc.;
2. strip joints and other erotic shows or stores;
3. being alone with your girlfriend for long periods of
   time;
4. young girls who talk all the time about marriage;
5. girls who are faster, sexually, than you are;
6. talking about sex with your girlfriend, except about
   how you want to remain pure until marriage;
7. friends who feel you are somehow less of a man
   because of your decision; and

8. alcohol, drugs, or anything else that will lower your defense systems. You should avoid these things anyway, but combining them with sexual situations is like combining fire and dynamite.

Find Someone to Be Accountable To

You need someone in your life, who is likely to remain in your life, who agrees with your position and is willing to discuss it with you on a frequent basis. It may be that you will also be helping the other person to stay in line sexually, or in some other part of his life where he needs help.

Your father or mother are perfectly suited to the task if you can be open with them about your sex life. Try talking to them even if you haven't before. You may be surprised at how happy they are that you brought it up. It could also be an older brother, uncle, pastor, or just a friend of the family. You will benefit greatly if this person's belief in abstinence is based on a strong moral foundation, rather than just the practical reasons.

Don't Touch—Or at Least Very Little

Keep the sexual part of your relationship with any girlfriend at the level of closed-mouth kissing and hand-holding. Anything else takes you beyond getting to know one another and friendly affection. French kissing, fondling one another, and the rest leads into passion. Once the passion gets started, it is very hard for us men to control our desires for more and more. I'm certain you will question my attitude about French kissing, but take my word for this one. This is the first step to runaway passion.

Will this part of the action plan be easy? No way. Is it possible? Absolutely. However, it takes character, discipline, and commitment.

Date in Groups

Or take your date to public places. Deserted beaches and private picnics are very romantic but also very dangerous.

Do Not Encourage Your Girlfriend to Take Birth Control

Do not carry condoms. The practical risks that come with unprotected sex reduce the likelihood that you will take the chance.

Read Other Material on Abstinence and Its Benefits

Without preaching about it, be prepared to clearly state your case any time the subject is discussed. You may or may not win arguments or converts. However, by knowing your position well, you will help yourself to stay on course.

Only Date Girls You Respect

First of all, this means you will need to get to know her well enough to be able to judge whether or not you respect her. Second, if you don't respect her, you are more likely to use her. Many boys and men tend to be users anyway, especially when it comes to women and sex. If you take someone out that you don't respect, you may feel there is less of a reason to worry about the potential negative consequences to her of any sexual activity. You may even think, "If she does it all the time anyway, what difference does it make if I get mine?"

To make matters worse, if you don't respect her, she may sense this and be more likely to push you to have sex with her. This might be because she wants you to like her and senses that you don't really care that much (girls have very strong intuition for these things). She may even feel she can get you to begin a long-term relationship if she "puts out." Either way, she will further break down your convictions by her sexual aggressiveness. And if you don't already know this, let me be the first to tell you: it is very difficult for a man to say "no" to a woman who is taking off her clothes and reaching for his private parts.

Peer Pressure

"I dare you. In fact, I double dare you." I don't think these words have changed in a century or more. Everyone, adults included, is under pressure from friends, enemies, and even strangers to act in certain ways. We want to dress, walk, talk, eat, and think in ways that we believe will cause others to like us.

It is a real shame that we act like this, because folks tend to like best those people who act the most natural and think for themselves. I always think of it as similar to hitting a baseball. Every time I concentrate real hard about the way

I'm standing, how I'm holding the bat, and if I'm looking cool, I end up swinging way too hard and miss for sure. But when I'm so well practiced that I'm standing naturally and comfortably in the batter's box, holding the bat as easily as I hold a toothbrush and thinking about what the pitcher is going to throw and where I'm going to hit it, BOOM! A solid hit.

And so it goes with how we act around our friends. Have you ever noticed that the person who is trying the hardest to be liked is liked the least? Who does everyone like best? The leader. He has the courage to do what he thinks is best. He decides what he wants to wear, and the followers copy him.

How does this get back to sex? You're going to spend a lot of time in the next few years talking about this subject with your friends. They are going to tell you what they have done with girls. Most of what they say is going to be exaggeration or outright lies. As they swap stories your turn will come. They'll be expecting you to tell about feeling somebody up or making it with your girlfriend. You will experience many different kinds of serious pressure at this point.

You'll feel pressured to tell them about things you've done, even if you haven't. This is lying, pure and simple. It's the worst kind of lying because it can lead to massive harm to others. If you say you have done things with a girl, when in fact you haven't, her reputation is affected. Others who hear of your success may wish to see if they can "score" with her. She will be horribly hurt that you have lied about her. In addition, others in the group will be further pressured by your claims to top your story with another lie (affecting another girl's reputation) or possibly to go out and actually become more sexually active. As a result, your friends or acquaintances may be affected by some or all of the previously mentioned tragic consequences.

You'll feel pressure to keep up with your friends. You will either increase your efforts with a current girlfriend to let you do more, or you will seek girls who are known to be easy. In either case, you will risk the girl's future and health, as well as your own.

You'll feel pressure to compromise your real values. It is hard to tell a group of guys that you don't believe in pre-marital sex. They are almost certain to laugh and call you sissy or worse. The truth is, however, that at least half of those in the group have either never had sex or maybe experienced it once. You may be shocked to discuss the issue with these same guys one at a time and find out they agree with you, or at least respect your stand.

The real test of your manhood is providing your group with solid reasons for abstaining. You should avoid sounding superior or condescending. Instead, make it clear to them how a few minutes of sexual delight can ruin their life and maybe several others at the same time.

I Think I Have Abnormal Sexual Thoughts

First, it is absolutely normal for teens to think they're abnormal. It goes with the territory to think that you are the only one who sometimes drools on his pillow, can't figure out geometry, or is really interested in computers. Our friends and the TV help us think we're weird by pointing to some types of actions as nerdy or geeky. No matter how you look or act, some people will think you are odd, and others will think you are terrific.

Even if it's normal to worry about being normal, it still isn't fun. Let's take a look at some of the areas of sexual abnormality and difficulty, and see if we can help you make a decision about just how normal you are.

Homosexuality

It is normal to worry about being less than a real man, even if you are a one hundred percent all-American male. You may have never even thought about whether you would enjoy more than a good handshake with a man, but you still might wonder if you're gay. Maybe your situation is different, however. You like girls. You are sexually aroused by girls. Still, you sometimes look at other guys and wonder about the other side of the fence. However, you have never done anything sexual with a male, you don't really plan to, and it isn't something that you think about all the time. These experiences do not denote homosexuality or even slight bi-sexuality. You are very likely still totally within the

normal range of behavior for a teen-ager or young adult.
However, you may be at risk, and you need to create a
barrier against that risk.

It is suspected that many young men will have one or
two homosexual experiences in their lives. These may not
involve intercourse but would still be looked upon as homosexual activity. You are most likely to have such an experience as the result of one of two situations. First, you and a
close friend who feels similarly may find yourselves experimenting sexually with your feelings during a sleep-over or
camp out. Second, you may accept the advances of a practicing homosexual who senses your uncertainty.

In either circumstance, but especially the second, you
are very likely to put yourself in serious jeopardy. You are
certainly aware of the potential for AIDS, but there are
numerous other sexually transmitted diseases that are at
epidemic levels within the homosexual community. In addition, you will carry around the emotional scar of this episode
for the rest of your life. I had one friend—of high intelligence
and well-adjusted—who attempted suicide, and nearly suc-
ceeded, after a single homosexual act. Finally, a practicing
homosexual will not be satisfied to lure you into a one-night
stand. He will want to introduce you to the gay community,
and the picture he paints may seem quite attractive.

If you feel that the description above fits you, be on
guard for any situation that could get out of hand. Don't
allow yourself to be alone with any guy you suspect is homosexual or bi-sexual. Resist any move that any other boy or
man makes that could be considered a pass or suggestion for
intimacy. Don't walk, *run* away from any talk of actually
experimenting with another man. If someone is bothering
you all the time, tell him that you will report his behavior to
your parents, school officials, or a trusted adult.

Possibly the following best describes you. You do not
feel aroused by women or girls. You can't figure out why
other guys are always talking about how big so-and-so's chest
is. You also can't help yourself from thinking about the body
of one of your male classmates. Worst of all, you do get
sexually aroused thinking about guys in the shower at school.
What do you do? *Change your thinking!*

Ignore the current idea of accepting this thinking as assurance of your sexual preference. If you have poor eyesight, you buy glasses. If you can't hear, you get a hearing aid. If you cry all the time and can't stop, you see a counselor. You don't say, with the weak evidence before you, "There's nothing that can be done, I'm proud to be gay." You need to find a counselor who believes you can be cured. The first one you visit may not believe this way, although nearly 70 percent of psychologists believe that homosexuality can be cured. Find one who will work to cure you, not help you accept your condition.

Stay away from homosexuals. They will try to keep you from getting cured. You will have a greater likelihood of slipping off the road to recovery. And in today's world, one slip can kill you!

Find a loving pastor in a church who will not condemn your problem but will love you out of it. Right-thinking Christians hate the sin but love the potential in the repentant sinner. Don't believe that portion of the gay rights propaganda which contends that those against homosexual conduct are afraid of homosexuals, or wish to exclude them from an equal role in society. Homosexual behavior is the problem, not the person who is struggling with homosexual desire.

Pornography and Voyeurism

Both of these problem areas have to do with your very natural desire to "look" at members of the opposite sex. Being interested in the bodies of young ladies is not a problem as long as it is kept within the bounds of mere attraction and doesn't cross the line into lust. The use of pornography is almost always related to lust. The act of looking through windows goes beyond lust into a kind of visual rape. Both of these activities are potentially very harmful to your self-esteem and your normal sexual future.

Up until this section, you may have been in close agreement with me. You may be able to see the practical and moral reasons for avoiding premarital sex, and almost every one of you will agree totally with the section on homosexuality. I know that it will be much harder to convince you to stay away from pornography. I know it is difficult, because I was once a user of such material.

It starts small with soft porn, but it builds quickly, as we will discuss. It is easy to rationalize that such material won't hurt you, but it most certainly will. You can stay away from it, but it takes character. For some reason our society has decided not to be very concerned about exploiting women and children in magazines, movies, and television.

My first argument against this type of material is that it is manipulative. Those who hope to make a buck are using this material with clear knowledge of its destructiveness to the pictured women and fully aware that the male consumer is also likely to be harmed. But their lust for profit totally overshadows any guilt they may feel. Publishers, producers and distributors also know that young men find it very difficult to stay away from pornography. They know that if a movie contains some nudity, teen-age boys and even old men like me are going to be curious to see what that particular star looks like undressed.

Well, I don't know about you, but I didn't like living under somebody else's control. I prefer to chart my own path, not walk blindly down an alley that some pusher takes me because he has control over me. Pornography can control you. It can cause you to lie to your parents, your girlfriend, and eventually your wife. It can result in your spending time and money that could much better be spent on school, work, sports, or friends.

As an adult, its many negative effects could interfere with your sexual relationship with your wife. First of all, she isn't going to like it a bit that you enjoy looking at those "other" nude women. She wants you to look at her and only her. Even if she never says anything, she will feel less loved and will be hurt that her body isn't enough to satisfy you. Second, you will appreciate your wife so much more if you aren't comparing her to all those perfectly posed and airbrushed women in the magazines.

So how do you know where to draw the line? Clearly, there is nothing wrong with looking at a girl or woman because you find her attractive, though you will want to avoid doing this when you are with your girlfriend or wife, because it is impolite and she will be offended. You should also avoid giving girls the "once over" or being obvious about your enjoyment in looking at them. Almost all women find this offensive.

The difficulty begins when your interest goes beyond the idea that this person is attractive and you start thinking about how much you'd like to see her undressed or to have sex with her. This is the point at which you dehumanize both her and yourself, and you put yourself in a position to be manipulated by her or by those who would profit from your desire to see indecent pictures.

Is it normal? You bet it is. It's also normal to want what someone else has enough to steal it. However, society still believes that stealing is wrong, if for no other reason than to protect our property. Society should be reconsidering its position on pornography if for no other reason than to protect our women (our moms, sisters, future wives).

Please stay away from pornography. You will end up wasting money and time.

I will only spend a short paragraph on voyeurism. It is illegal to invade someone else's privacy for any purpose, but when that purpose is to watch them undress or bathe, it is a great injustice to that person. If you have ever done this or have even seriously considered it, imagine what you would want to do to the boy or man whom you caught watching your sister, mom, or girlfriend.

Respect for Women

Do you respect the girls in your group of friends? Are there young women outside of your social circle whom you respect? How about the girls you see on TV and in movies? If you can't readily agree with the following statements, it is hard to imagine that any fair judge would say that you respect women.

1. I refuse to look at pictures of naked girls in magazines, movies, and video tapes.
2. I never use vulgar language or discuss sexually explicit subjects with my casual female friends.
3. I never touch a female acquaintance in any way that might be seen as sexual.

4. I would never go out with a girl with the intention of having sex.

5. I never force my desires on a girlfriend. My intentions in our relationship are getting to know her, meeting her needs, and seeing how she might meet mine.

6. It is my intention to have sex only within marriage.

7. I would never strike a woman or abuse her in any way.

8. I would never discuss the sexual aspects of the relationship I have with my girlfriend with others.

9. If I were to have sex with my girlfriend, and she were to become pregnant, I would be willing to marry her and have the child in order to protect her and the child from abortion and/or poverty. If this were not a viable option, I would help her put the baby up for adoption.

If you can pass the above test, there is hope for the future of America. If you can convince your friends of the importance of such respect for women, a future generation might not have to fear that their daughters will be the victims of rape, incest, sexual disease, abortion, out-of-wedlock pregnancy, or other consequences of sexually inappropriate behavior.

A Final Thought

Making love with your wife is one of God's greatest gifts. Only a few of life's other experiences can possibly compare. Gaining this gift in your life is well worth the sacrifice of a few moments of pleasure where sexual release is the only objective. You may or may not be able to influence the actions or thinking of your friends and associates with regard to their decisions about their sexual lives. However, you do have complete control over your own actions and thinking. It is up to you how you lead your own life.

You will decide whether or not you will be responsible for someone else's harm due to your sexual behavior. You will have no one else to blame for the guilt and shame you will feel if you are a party to their contracting a sexual disease, becoming pregnant, having an abortion, or even dying. It's totally up to you.

Will it be easy to abstain until marriage? *No.* Will there

be pressure to become sexually active from friends, the entertainment industry, and maybe even your girlfriend? *Yes.* Can it be done? *Yes.* It's being done every single day. What will it take from you? First it takes a decision. Then you will need to develop character, commitment, and discipline. Only you know if you have the courage to overcome your own desires and the pressure of friends and situations. Only you know if you have the discipline to make and keep a commitment that can so incredibly benefit your life and the life of others. Only you know whether or not you care enough about others not to allow your passion to potentially destroy their lives.

Maybe you have already been sexually active. Possibly you are already hooked on porn. Maybe you are already involved in homosexual activity. Now is the time to stop! Yes, you will undoubtedly suffer the consequences of this past behavior. Yes, you will be haunted by these parts of your life for some time to come. However, by stopping now, you can eliminate the possibility of hurting still other innocent people. You can begin to heal your own emotions, a process that will occur with the passage of time.

The best way to help yourself deal with past or present sexual error and to avoid future harmful and immoral sexual activity is to come under the saving grace of Jesus Christ. If you would like to find out how Christ can come into your life and provide you with the wisdom, desire, and grace to deal with these issues, visit your local church and talk with the pastor.

If you have not already read the previous chapter for teen-age girls, I recommend you read it as carefully as you have this one. The more you learn about how women act and why, the better you will be able to create a lasting relationship. Be certain to read the chapter addressed to all men. After all, you are on the verge of being one. Then read the final three chapters to learn what you can do to help make a better future for your younger brothers and sisters and the kids you'll someday father in a loving, committed marriage.

SEVEN

An Eye-Opening Document for All Mothers

❖

A mother explained . . . her unwed maternity this way: "It is selfish, but this was something I needed to do for me."
> by Barbara Dafoe Whitehead
> "Dan Quayle Was Right"
> *Atlantic Monthly*, April 1993

Adult males have been taking all the heat for the breakdown in the social fabric and the failure of families during the past thirty years. If you read chapter 8, "An Open Letter to Fathers," you can see that I have not cut them any slack either. I would agree that the lack of responsibility exhibited by fathers today is pitiful. I am appalled by the disrespect apparent in many men's relationships with women, whether in the home, the social context, or the office.

I am, however, equally disgusted with many in the adult female population. I said in 1970 that the role confusion created by the women's movement would produce a disaster for marriage and male/female relationships, and I am sorry to say that I underestimated the resulting disruption. The divorce rate today doesn't begin to describe the depth of the breakdown in the way husbands and wives, boyfriends and girlfriends, and men and women in general interact with one another.

The effect of women wanting to be like men, and simultaneously promoting the feminization of men, left both sexes at a loss for ways to act around one another. Because men and women are biologically quite different and have decidedly diverse needs, the effort to adapt to a new social order failed miserably. Some men and some women actually changed substantially to fit the new idea of how they should act. In many cases, however, this meant they were no longer fulfilling the needs of their spouses. Ironically, many women who bought into the idea that their husbands should be more sensitive and nurturing were the very ones who needed their family to be headed by a strong, self-assured leader. (Yes, it is possible for a man to be sensitive, nurturing, strong, and self-assured. But show me more than a dozen examples in the history of the human race who have been able to do all of these things well.)

Others tried to change and failed, leaving them with lowered self-esteem and with a spouse who felt the failure was due to a lack of effort. A large percentage didn't make any effort to change. If one spouse believed in the principles of change, that spouse would be dissatisfied with the mate who wouldn't try, regardless of whether his or her real needs were being met. Let's take a look at an example. In the fifties there were very few women who wanted to enter the work force. Those who did usually had to deal with a husband who "didn't believe in it." The man saw himself as the "breadwinner" and felt his wife should be home taking care of the children and running the household. If the wife's feelings were strong enough, there probably was a resulting conflict.

As women became more convinced that they should pursue careers, this conflict grew and grew. The man was left with a choice. One: he could adapt to the new way of thinking and encourage his wife's career. Many did. This left a number of these men feeling inadequate; a number of the women, philosophically believing a career was a good idea, felt as if their husbands were less a man. Later, as couples began to depend on two incomes, working wives came to feel trapped in their jobs. Even if they decided that they would prefer to become full-time mothers or homemakers, societal and financial pressure kept them from taking that option.

Two: the man could, as others did so grudgingly, accept the change. Some agreed to the idea of their wives working but hated the idea. Many of these men came to appreciate the better standard of living their wives' incomes produced but not the extra pressures their wives felt in trying to be a "superwife" or "supermom." These situations often resulted in unresolved conflict, the most common precursor to relationship breakdown.

Three: the man could clearly state his disagreement with his spouse's desire to have a career. If she was strongly desirous of working outside the home, she would have to either grudgingly accept his decision or take a job contrary to his wishes. Either result would be a clear road to major conflict—and it *was* in a number of households.

Meanwhile, a wife who really didn't want to work felt pressure from society or her husband to enter the work force. Society insisted women could only be truly successful if they had a career. Her husband might have agreed with society's opinion or merely felt the financial pressure of trying to keep up with other two-income families. In either case, the wife was caught in yet another trap.

As relationship roles broke down, so did marriages. As confusion increased as to how each was to act, children became confused as to proper sexual identity and therefore experienced confusion about their own. When people are confused about who they are and what they are supposed to do, they become neurotic or even psychotic. Is it any wonder that there is so much dysfunction in our society?

The role identity confusion was not the only misguided effort of the women's movement. Along with men, women have become totally self-centered, wiping out the historic self-sacrificing image of mothers. Today, we have mothers who rarely see the children that they don't abort.

Tough talk? How else could one describe the incredible state of motherhood today? For a large percentage of the population today, a woman's first decision as a new mother is what to do with an unwanted baby. How can this first experience result in anything positive? The choices are traumatic in their life-and-death finality: Kill it, give it up, or keep it.

The least emotionally troubling of these is to keep it—
that is, to keep an unwanted child. The very idea of an
"unwanted child" is virtually a creation of this generation.
Certainly there were those in other times who gave up their
children for adoption or even had abortions due to difficult
circumstances. But the babies themselves were not unwanted.
How can we imagine ourselves to be civilized when our
women are the first to describe their own offspring as unwanted? Or give the reasons they give for why they are
unwanted:

1. Inconvenient at this time;
2. Out of wedlock;
3. Can't afford it;
4. Wrong sex;
5. Can't "handle" it;
6. Might be handicapped;
7. Husband or boyfriend doesn't want it;
8. Too young;
9. Interfere with my social life;
10. Interfere with my schooling.

This attitude is bound to continue after the birth. It
should come as no surprise that babies who were unwanted
may have been gotten rid of, but even the ones that were
"wanted" are going to be inconvenient, expensive, and possibly difficult or even handicapped.

In other words, children come second or even third in
mom's life. Career, social life, the gym, and even TV will
successfully compete for mom's attention. Why does Johnny
have low self-esteem? His own mother cares more about the
television than about him. Why should he feel good about
himself? He may even be told that he was a surprise, unwanted, or a great inconvenience. He may be told that if it
weren't for him, she could have (fill in the blank) . . . ! He
may be told, and will believe anyway, that his parents' divorce was his fault. Then he may be told that his baseball
practices are interfering with his mother's dating career. It's
a pretty grim picture, mom.

What's the answer? How can we change the hearts of
millions and millions of women who have been taught that
they should put themselves and their desires first? Even if we

can change their hearts, how long will it take for their behavior to follow? And then, how much longer to undo the damage?

Four Challenges

First, throw off the horrible bondage imposed by the women's liberation movement. Men and women are different. No woman should ever be denied equal access to any aspect of what life or society has to offer. However, that doesn't mean that women should feel compelled to do things men do or do them in a man's way.

If a woman feels more comfortable working in her home to provide the best possible environment for her husband and children, then she should not feel any pressure from society to do otherwise. If she takes time away from her career for child-rearing, or works shorter hours in order to maximize her time with her children, she should make that decision with full knowledge of the impact it will have on her career, but without condemnation from those who believe she has somehow short-changed herself.

It's OK to be feminine and all that it implies. You should act in ways that are comfortable to you and in keeping with your values. Don't act like a man in order to fit in. Crude language is never appropriate, but it takes on an even more offensive aspect when uttered by a woman in mixed company. If you believe that a man (or even your husband) should show respect and deference to you by opening doors, by all means let him know that you appreciate these niceties.

If you don't want a career, or to work outside the home, don't pretend that you do. Believe it or not, many women get great satisfaction out of cooking, cleaning—even ironing. Why should sitting in front of a computer screen all day creating invoices or writing reports have a higher value than providing care and nurture for your own offspring who are the future of our nation?

Allow your husband to be a man. Don't pressure him to become more nurturing or fond of housework. If you and he were to have all the same skills, interests, and personality traits, why would a family need both of you? The fact is, the family benefits from the differences that you bring. Henry

Higgins may have humorously asked the question, "Why can't a woman be more like a man," in the song from *My Fair Lady*, but today's women are seriously asking men to be more like women. There is no advantage to that proposition either, and the disadvantages have already made themselves known.

Second, be prepared to sacrifice for your family, especially your children. Do you doubt for one minute that your husband would march off to war tomorrow, fully prepared to sacrifice his life, if your community was in danger of attack? Would he, without hesitation, dive into dangerous waters to pull you or one of your children from danger? Would he shield any one of you from an attack with his own body? Almost all of you can answer a confident "Yes!" Why then is it too much to ask the mothers of America to sacrifice their time, career, emotional commitment, even their present happiness to insure that their children have the best opportunity to maximize their potential?

Will it be worth it? If this question is asked, the questioner has already missed the point of sacrifice.

In the times prior to 1965, most parents without question willingly, even happily, sacrificed for their children. Society dictated that if you brought children into the world, you had a responsibility to them, the community, the nation, and God to do whatever you could to create a better and more secure life for them than you enjoyed.

About this same time, society decided to experiment with drugs, sex, alternative lifestyles, and other hedonistic behavior (devoted to pleasure). Parents now thought only of themselves and started to see children as a nuisance. This same idea continues to permeate our thinking today. As President Clinton takes over the White House, family issues revolve around more "day care" so that more moms can work; "family leave" so that moms can be home at least for emergencies and dads can be around more for the first six weeks of life; and "abortion on demand" throughout the pregnancy so that moms can get rid of unwanted children. Those who support such measures have the gall to call them "family values."

What does sacrifice mean?

1. Staying home and giving full attention to your children at least until they are in full-time school; being home when they are.
2. Meaning perhaps you can't afford certain things you'd like to have;
3. Perhaps always having less "things" or career success than those who do not interrupt their careers;
4. Less social life, and the social life that is left may be much more low key; less or no alcohol, earlier hours, different friends;
5. Evaluation of your attitudes and habits to take into consideration their effect on your children's future: cigarettes, sexually oriented materials, alcohol, language, irresponsible financial habits, and ways of relating to your spouse, friends, and the kids;
6. A willingness to be your kids' parent, not their friends: effective discipline, training in values, saying "NO," even though this may mean your kids may not like you for a day or so;
7. Time, time, and more time; involvement in their activities, school, homework, church groups, and sports;
8. Caring about them; being willing to step back from your own immediate needs, wants, or feelings in order to do what is best for them;
9. Working at your marriage; staying in a marriage that isn't "totally satisfying" or that might even be "unhappy" to provide stability in their lives.

Third, protect them from harm. Would you let your two-year-old play on a busy street? Your second-grader drive the car? Your preteen spend his evenings at a bar? In fact, you're far more protective than that. Your two-year-old can't even cross a quiet residential street without you. The second-grader is limited as to where he can ride his bike. The preteen can't attend a party where alcohol will be served.

Why then, do you allow your local school to teach your fifth-grader that homosexuality is an acceptable alternative lifestyle? Why do you allow your thirteen-year-old to watch television programs that convey the idea that virginity is out of style? Why do you stand by as your high school passes out condoms to your teen-agers?

Have you told your children that "all sex should be reserved for the marriage bed"? Have you explained to them that "French kissing can be the match that creates the flames that result in pregnancy or VD"? Have you admonished your daughters that "boys will use all kinds of tactics to seduce you"? Have you taught your boys to "respect women"?

Fourth, practice and preach commitment, fidelity, honesty, discipline, perseverance, honor, graciousness, responsibility, integrity, and selflessness. Provide them with a biblically based code of values that starts with the Ten Commandments and ends with Christ's commands to love one another as yourself, and to love the Lord your God with all your heart, soul, and might.

You were probably taught in school that there are no absolute values. Your parents at home and your Sunday School teachers at church taught all the values in the above paragraph. Today your kids are being told at school that they can decide values for themselves. If they don't attend a church which teaches values, and if you aren't telling them about the golden rule, why is anyone surprised when they don't do what they are told? Should it be a shock that our adult men are harassing women in the workplace, failing to provide support for their children after divorce, or beating up their girlfriends and wives?

Moms Are Very Special People

Many of the specific actions you can take to protect your kids from the immoral and destructive elements of society that are all around them can be found in chapter 8, "An Earnest Warning to All Fathers." Please read these and discuss them with your mate. The two of you need to agree about how and when to put each of these ideas into practice.

If you are a single mom, it is even more critical that you read that chapter, because the entire burden of those actions has fallen to you. In either case, you still have the special position in the house of "mother." There are few who would disagree with the idea that you are the backbone of the family. The man may be the head and hopefully he provides leadership. However, if he fails in his natural role—whether due to death, divorce, abandonment, incompetence, or indifference—you, the backbone, have to do it all.

For the purposes of this chapter, doing it all means explaining the facts of life, not just the part about how babies are made, but all the other parts described in chapter 9. As mentioned there, your big, strong, successful husband may be good at many things but have a very hard time telling your preteen daughter about sexuality and all that goes with it.

Teach Your Sons to Respect Women and Girls

The historical double standard may keep your husband from telling your sons that they should restrain their sexual urges until marriage. Or, if he does give the speech, it may be with a wink. This same husband may be quite good at telling his daughters about the horrible end that awaits them should they experiment with their sexuality, yet he may believe that the worst thing that might happen to his son is an itchy case of crabs. Hopefully, you will both make the case for the Bible's clear teaching that fornicators will not inherit the kingdom of God.

Mom, believe it or not, your son practically worships the ground you walk on. Sometimes, he may not be able to please you or follow your dictates because he just doesn't have what it takes. But it is the rare son who doesn't want to please his mom.

From this base you should be able to provide him with an understanding of how important it is to treat all girls and women with respect. Hopefully, as a little boy, he was taught not to hit women, that girls go first, and that certain types of touching are not allowed under any circumstances. Shouldn't it be just as appropriate to tell a twelve-year-old boy that as he begins to become interested in girls, he must continue, or even increase, his respectful behavior in dealing with the ladies in his life? Some new elements that might complement his earlier childhood teachings might include:

1. Courteous behavior such as holding doors open, walking on the traffic side of the sidewalk, standing when a lady joins a group, introducing girls first, and all of the other aspects of deference that have been ignored for thirty years but should never be overlooked.

2. "No" means "no!" We would be wise to teach our young ladies not to use "no" in a coy or flirtatious

manner. Therefore, if men are to be taught that a woman means it when she says "no," it is critical that their experience bear that out.

3. There seems to be a lot of confusion today among even the most mannered of young men about what kinds of touching are allowed in casual relationships. While it would be difficult to go into great detail here, in general it would seem to be important to tell an adolescent boy to restrict his touching to hands and forearms.

4. Our society has always allowed and barely discouraged "locker room language" and off-color stories among men. However one might feel about this type of behavior when limited to same-sex groups, it is totally inappropriate among mixed singles, reducing respect and knocking down barriers to intimacy.

5. This could be a great time to reinforce the idea that men never strike women.

6. Age twelve might be a little early to talk about wandering eyes, but a mother may want to try to be on the lookout for behavior which might create the timing for such a discussion. A boy cannot very well show respect for a girl while he undresses her with his eyes.

7. You will surely want to prohibit the purchase or use of pornographic material, and it would be an excellent idea to discuss the potential for harm that comes with such products.

As your young man grows up you will need to have additional conversations with him that are specific to the circumstances he is dealing with at any given time. Because kids will experiment with their sexuality at vastly different ages, you will have to be vigilant in your observation of what might be going on in their lives and minds. The secret is to be interested in their life—not prying, not judging, and especially not condemning. In most cases your children will be very desirous of discussing what is happening to them. They are particularly uncertain during these teen years and are looking for any hard ground they can find. Especially in the early adolescent years, they still trust your judgment.

Clearly, it is easier to get the girls to be open and communicative about these tender issues than it is the boys. You may also find that one of your children may have an easier time going to one parent than to the other. Try to keep your resentment in check if your daughter finds it easier to talk to her dad, and encourage your husband not to take it personally if your son is more open with you. In these times of moral relativism, it is critical that you explain to your children the difference between those ideas, attitudes, and behaviors that are absolutely right or wrong and those which do require, or may be colored by, our own evaluation and interpretation.

For instance, in the area of sex, it is a moral absolute that people should not engage in intercourse outside of marriage. This is a basic tenet of Judeo-Christian belief and is found just as clearly in almost every other culture in history. On the other hand, so-called French kissing may be a very bad idea for unmarried individuals because it may fan the flame of emotions and lead to sexual sin; however, by itself French kissing is not absolutely wrong.

Therefore, in explaining your position to your teens, your ability to point out the differences between acts that are "wrong" and those that are "advised against" will greatly increase your credibility. Teen-agers want to have freedom to make decisions affecting their lives, and thus, the idea of moral relativism is very popular. On the other hand, all humans of any age find strength, security, and self-confidence in knowing what their limits are. This then can be one of your greatest gifts to your children—drawing the distinction and clearly stating the boundaries.

What specifically should you and/or your husband say to your son as he moves through the teen years?

1. As mentioned above, once he is old enough to deal clearly with this area, he should be told in the clearest possible language that sex prior to or outside of marriage is absolutely forbidden, attacking it at several levels:

a) Morally—Turn to the Scriptures and history and provide the overwhelming evidence of the almost universal ban on premarital and extramarital sex. There is good reason why both God and man have seen fit to place this issue on the same level as murder and thievery.

b) *Practically*—He may be more impressed by the financial consequences of paying for a child for eighteen or more years than he is by the potential of contracting a disease. Teen-agers, especially boys, commonly believe they are invincible.

c) *Emotionally*—Many young men who consider themselves both invincible and beyond the moral constructs of either God or man can be appealed to on the level of social responsibility, the secular school's last remaining absolute value. Pointing to the potential harm he can cause for his girlfriend, especially through transmission of painful and debilitating diseases, may have a major impact.

d) *Hope*—Another very useful approach is explaining the once-in-a-lifetime opportunity for spiritual oneness that can only be part of a relationship between two individuals who have exclusively shared their love with one another.

2. In the context of this discussion the question will usually arise, "If I shouldn't have sex with my girlfriend, how far can we go?" Here you have the opportunity to offer advice and allow him to make judgments. Anyone who has been in an intimate relationship with another person can relate to the passions that build with each level of sexual play. You can hope to keep your son out of harm's way by offering these possible approaches:

a) try to avoid any intimacy beyond a chaste kiss and holding hands;

b) avoid those places and opportunities for being alone and unchaperoned ("parking," picnics in remote areas, weekends together planned with the best intentions);

c) be accountable to someone—an older friend, counselor, pastor, or respected relative. (The purpose of such accountability is for the mentor to ask his charge at regular meetings straightforward questions about his behavior so that he can help the younger to avoid traps and pitfalls.

3. In these times it would also be prudent to have a hardball discussion about homosexuality. Since teen-agers who are perfectly "straight" may sometimes question their sexual feeling about same-sex individuals. Point out that only two persons in one hundred will actually find those feelings to be so predominant that they will act out in whole or in

part homosexual behavior, begin this talk by making it clear that it is common to have some feelings of this type and explain that the acting out of these feelings is sinful and has been taboo in virtually every human society. Help them understand that it may be likened to adultery, drug addiction, or other human frailties that require, if persistent, a talk with a counselor. Like many other aspects of human physiology or psychology, the earlier such inclinations are discovered, the more likely that treatment will be successful. If you bury your head in the sand, despite your deepest suspicions, your adult homosexual child may have been so indoctrinated by his peers that he will lack the desire to consider treatment.

4. A commonly forgotten subject in the "son" talk is the woman-as-vamp. It is always a part of the daughter's warning that men will use every move in the book to get her into bed. However, it is not news that many young women will do anything to hold on to their man or bring him to the altar. The boy is holding back sexually, but the young lady is unbuttoning her blouse or touching him suggestively. The boy needs every bit as much warning as to how to deal with this situation—maybe even more—as with those spurred by his own desires. After trying to talk to his girlfriend, apprising her of his intention to remain a virgin until marriage and why, convincing her it has nothing to do with how he feels about her, and using the "slow down" tactics discussed earlier, your son may need to simply end the relationship. One of the greatest defenses is to end the discussion during a passionate moment and go home to cool off, bringing up the issue again when there is no chance of hurrying into a bad decision.

5. Imagine the benefits to the next generation of marriages if this generation of mothers explained to their sons what women want. Moms, talk to them about a wife's somewhat lower concern for the physical side of lovemaking and the rather greater interest in the romantic, emotional aspects. Tell your son that it is hard for a woman to be excited about lovemaking when she is tired, upset, anxious, or hasn't heard a romantic word for six weeks. Tell him that women never hear the words "I love you" too often, or that they

never tire of receiving flower or cards. I'm sure you have a few more ideas. You could make a future daughter-in-law worship her mother-in-law by passing on a few tips that won't hurt your son during his dating years either.

6. There needs to be constant retraining in the areas of respect, physical abuse, manners, pornography, and inappropriate touching in casual acquaintances.

7. I would recommend that you make it clear that if your young man makes a mistake in any of these areas, even a big one like getting a girlfriend pregnant, that you want him to come to you with the problem. He needs to believe that you will not condemn him or make his life miserable because of his shortfall; that doesn't mean that there will not be consequences. The key here is that you want to be able to work together with him on a solution.

Teach Your Daughters to Respect Themselves

Today's young women, after twenty years of liberation, increased educational opportunity, and entry into almost every kind of career, are experiencing ever lowering levels of self-respect. Dr. James Dobson, one of the most prolific writers on social-psychological issues of our day, took an informal poll of over 10,000 women, trying to determine what about themselves was their greatest concern. Overwhelmingly they answered that they experienced feelings of low self-worth.

How can the most far-reaching liberation movement in history be accompanied by the liberated group having less self-esteem? More importantly, how can you, as a parent, build self-respect into your teen-age daughters?

Without getting too philosophical, one reason free societies sometimes long for a dictator is because they grow weary of the price of freedom—making choices. Liberty has a price. In addition to this general increase in anxiety due to the choices that women have today, a teen-age girl's relationships with men of all ages are more likely to be devastating to her sense of worth than they are to be uplifting.

First, nearly 50 percent of our teen-agers are partially or totally estranged from their fathers. Even those whose dad is at home commonly feel that he is far from supportive. If the

young woman can't even count on her father for unconditional love, how can she possibly trust her boyfriend? Amazingly, she does trust him in an immature, desperate way.
Many long so for the instinctual male shoulder to cry on or
the security of a man's hug that they latch on to any man
who looks at them twice.

From her obvious display of no foundation of self-respect and a strong need to be loved, even a young teen-age
boy can see that he is in a position of power, setting the
young woman up for disaster. At the very least, it is unlikely
that this relationship will last long. Even though she has
given him everything, he eventually rejects her. Her self-
respect dives, and she will commonly repeat this pattern
over and over.

That brings us to how you, as a mother, can help your
daughter see herself as worthy of respect from others and,
therefore, from herself. One of the most important ways is
to make certain that by the time she is ten or eleven there
is an adult male in her life who will love her unconditionally—one who will give her his time, energy, and direction.

Of course, the best candidate for this job is her natural
father. If you are still married to him, you must make him
aware of how important it is for him to give her total emotional support. In most cases, he will be the first man she
loves romantically.

If the biological father is no longer in the home, I can't
be emphatic enough that you work overtime to keep up his
visitations all through her teen years. You may want to explain the reason why. No matter how loving a stepdad may
be, if the biological dad is still in the picture, she needs him
to reaffirm her value, and she needs it badly.

If there is a stepfather, but no biological dad in the
picture, the stepdad has his work cut out for him. He will
need to be a super-stepdad to weather her insecurity-driven
rejection, but he is her best hope of reaching adulthood with
the ability to relate well with men and, eventually, her own
future mate.

Finally, if there is no man in the picture, you would do
very well to try to find an uncle, neighbor, preacher, or
someone else who can fill this part. Obviously, your choice

must be judicious since bringing an adult male into this type of relationship can backfire. You must look for someone who has the maturity to handle the assignment without handling the merchandise.

Another important way to build self-respect is to encourage her to act like she already has it. You will want to make it clear to your daughter that she should handle herself in such a way that it is obvious to others that she has a clear understanding of who she is and where she stands on important issues. By doing so, she will receive the kind of feedback that will reinforce these behaviors. For example, imagine walking into a store that sells a technical product such as a stereo. If you have basic knowledge about the purchase, you discuss the various options with the salesperson in a confident manner, making it clear what you want and don't want, and he will likely treat you with dignity. He is unlikely to try to sell you expensive, unnecessary options that you don't need. This is because he senses your self-confidence and doesn't want to appear to be unsophisticated in his own field—he unconsciously seeks approval from you. On the other hand, if you come in and communicate from the beginning that you don't know anything about the product, what you should buy, or how much to spend, and also appear spineless, he will likely try to sell you the whole store. He will not respect you enough to worry about your opinion of him or his statements.

It works this way with personal relations also. If you act as if you have clear feelings about the way you conduct your affairs, those who interact with you are very likely to respect your beliefs, opinions, and methods. As you sense their respect, you will feel greater confidence in yourself and your beliefs, opinions, and methods. [*Final note*: There is a difference between someone respecting you and agreeing with you. When someone disagrees with your position, don't mistake this for their not respecting you. If you are consistent, not hypocritical, you will gain the respect of most people, whether or not they agree with you.]

What can your daughter do to give the appearance of having self-respect even while still developing it? (We will limit this to the context of relationships with men.)

1. *Dress modestly.* Like it or not, impressions are based to a large extent on appearance. How else can we account for the interest in "dress for success" books or the monumental amounts of money that are spent on clothing, cosmetics, plastic surgery, hair transplants, and work-out videos? Shouldn't it be easy, therefore, to figure that if a woman or girl dresses in such a way as to call attention to her sexuality, she will be seen as flaunting that part of her being because she feels it is the only part of her likely to attract men? If she feels this way, she clearly has no self-respect. If her dress implies it, it doesn't matter if she truly feels it; those who are evaluating her as a potential friend, associate, employee, or date will believe it and assume that she has no self-respect. Even those who are able to look beyond a person's appearance in making a decision about them, will still be persuaded that a young woman who is dressing immodestly lacks self-respect.

Mom, if you lay down the law to a fourteen-year-old about modesty in dress, fighting her tooth and nail about each outfit you judge to be "over the line," she will likely rebel. However, if you patiently point out the reasoning above—yes, over and over—your daughter is more likely to receive the idea and act on it. Remember also the various aspects of how to sit, bend over, cross legs, etc., along with other material covered in the section addressed to teen-age girls. You should certainly read this section as well for other ideas to discuss with your daughter.

2. *Don't touch or allow yourself to be touched.* This issue breaks down into two parts: touching and talking. Women who touch their male friends and acquaintances in certain ways clearly send signals of low self-respect. In particular this would include touching casual acquaintances on the rear end, upper leg, nape of the neck, or bare chest, or running fingers through the hair. Any "safe" touching (e.g., on back of the hand, forearm, shoulder, or face) needs to be discreet and infrequent, or it too can become too flirtatious.

In the same way, a girl should not allow herself to be touched on the rear end or leg, or to be massaged anywhere. Moreover, she should always be in control of any other type of touching that she doesn't want. If she doesn't want a boy

to put his arm around her, she should make it clear that this
attention is unwanted. The first time this can be mentioned
in a kind and pleasant way. The second time, the reaction
should make her position unmistakable.

3. *Guard the tongue.* Is there any part of the human drama
that results in more problems than the tongue? If the answer
is no, it is doubly so for the ladies in our society. Is this an
unfair stereotype? No, it is an undisputable fact of nature.
Women speak more words per day than men and the more
our mouths are open, the more opportunity there is to
insert our foot.

One of the fastest ways your daughter can destroy her
reputation is through the way she talks. She can very quickly
increase or decrease the respect she gets from boys and men
and their perception of her self-respect.

First and foremost, any discussion of intimate aspects of
sex should be totally off limits. Does this mean that a young
woman should not engage in debates or discussion of the
issues raised in this book? No, but it does mean that if the
discussion moves away from serious consideration of issues
and moves into subject matter that might be titillating to
either party, the line has been crossed. Preteens and teens
should probably stay as far away as possible from any discussion about sex with a friend of the opposite gender. Talking
about these issues in mixed company has a way of reducing
mystery and courting unfortunate possibilities.

Also on the taboo list should be off-color remarks, language, and jokes. I will be happy to change my position on
this if I learn of one instance in my own life or in the lives
of my friends and acquaintances in which a girl or woman
has enhanced her reputation or respect among those around
her through the use of "locker room" talk. Does that mean
that a girl won't find herself the center of attention because
she talks dirty? No, she may very well become quite popular
for such talk, but will she be respected? Not in my experience. She would undoubtedly become even more popular if
she did a strip tease every day during lunch break, but
respect is different from popularity.

4. *Take clear stands on various issues of the day and then
consistently hold to these.* The fastest way to destroy respect is

to stake out such a position and then be seen to be hypocritical or wildly inconsistent.

Set Up Hedges of Protection for Your Kids

One of the hardest things you have to do as a parent is to say "No." (Even harder are consoling your daughter after she's been raped, dealing with the shock after she's told you she is HIV positive, or identifying her lifeless body at the morgue after a night of party.) The hardest thing a kid has to hear from you is that same word. When your kids reach age ten or so, there is a subtle change in their brain chemistry that allows them to begin thinking for themselves. At that point in their life, it is no longer enough to say no, and it can often be counterproductive. Rather, you will want to develop in their thinking the basis for good decision-making, then monitor their judgment during these early years while you can still stop them from major errors.

Jerry Jensen, an author writing on men's issues, used the concept of hedges. A hedge can be seen as a protective device we put in place to keep evil out, and to keep ourselves from unrestricted movement toward that evil. For example, one hedge that I would require is that no friends of either sex be allowed to stay in the house when there is no adult home. This would be true for any age and for both sons and daughters. You will undoubtedly agree that having a friend of the opposite sex in the house without supervision is an open door to trouble. I would argue that the same goes for same-gender friends. I have seen many examples where two or three of the sweetest fifteen-year-old girls in the world create unbelievable havoc when left alone for more than an hour.

However, and here is the key to hedge-building, if you say to your son, "No. You can't have Linda over while we're away tonight," an argument is bound to follow with hurt all over the place. If, on the other hand, you sit down and examine the potential results with your child, he will usually concede that the opportunity for a bad result is there.

The most likely argument to this more orderly approach is "Gee, it seems like you don't trust me." In most cases you can diffuse this response by explaining that you do trust him, but you don't trust the situation and recognize that we all sometimes fail to resist temptation. Point out that you trust him to turn his homework in every day, but you also allow TV only after the homework is done. Here are some other hedges we should put up around our kids that they can see as protection, rather than mere restrictions on freedom, or evidence of lack of trust.

1. Similar to above, agree that they should not stay at a friend's house without one of the parents home.

2. Agree that they won't be able to attend unchaperoned parties or parties at homes in which the parents are known to allow drinking, drugs, sex, or other unacceptable behavior. Call ahead and ask the parents their views.

3. Agree that they will avoid association with other kids who drink, do drugs, smoke, drive recklessly, participate in unacceptable sexual behavior, cut school, or are known to behave lawlessly. Suggest to your kids that they share the problems of their friends with you. Assure them that you will not interfere unless they want you to or a very dangerous situation develops. However, agree that if a friend is likely to influence them in a way that will be against their best interest, they will distance themselves from that friend.

I'm sure you will come up with some of your own hedges. This is not to say that there aren't some areas of their lives where you will make a law rather than agree on a hedge. However, in some of these sensitive situations, you may have much greater compliance and maintain a better relationship by using this method.

It would appear that women in Western culture have been dealt a full hand; no woman I know would deny that. What has been denied for a while is the necessity of our women playing that hand fully. It is time for you to accept responsibility for your actions and drop the false god of self-actualization.

If you don't respect yourself enough to refuse sex outside of marriage—don't cry when men don't respect you. If you create a child—birth it. If you birth a child—put your whole being into raising it. If you marry—take your vows seriously. Be prepared to sacrifice, protect, and nurture your family even when you don't particularly feel like it. You will be fighting against peers, schools, and the media who are currently sending you and your children a different message. Please be certain to read the final chapters of this book which suggest a possible way to bring all those in our culture back to agreement on sexual standards and roles.

EIGHT

An Earnest Warning to All Fathers

─────────────── ❖ ───────────────

Sleep around all you want, but don't get married until you establish your career.

Debra Koenig, an attorney taking part on a panel addressing seventh-grade girls as part of Take Our Daughters to Work Day

Santa Monica Outlook,
1 May 1993

Today's average father is the most miserable excuse for a man in the history of civilization. Future generations will surely look back on these men as not only irresponsible, but lacking in basic character, as well. You need proof?

1. Today we have millions of unwed mothers whose impregnators deny fatherhood, or take no responsibility for the care and nurture of the results of their moment of pleasure.

2. We have countless mothers and children who have been left by adulterous men, or men who needed to "find themselves," or who were unwilling to "work it out" with their wives. Once having abandoned their families, these same "fathers" commonly failed to provide reasonable child support and/or emotional support in the form of frequent visits, phone calls, and letters. Our forefathers felt that this responsibility even passed to the relatives of a father in the case of his death. Today, many of our men are so weak, they just run and hide.

3. Many (over half) of today's fathers are standing idly by while their daughters are assaulted by men, both young and old, by dates, strangers, and criminals, and by uncles, cousins, stepdads, brothers, and granddads. A real man wouldn't sleep until he brought to justice any boy or man who even improperly touched his daughter, much less slept with her, impregnated her, or beat her up! How can any father fail to do less to protect his innocent daughter? Most have been emasculated by a culture which calls on a man to cry but not to defend his family.

4. Men hide behind "sensitivity to women's issues" arguments while their own grandchildren are ripped from the womb, piece by piece, or killed in salt solution. Just over fifty years ago, their fathers fought a valiant battle against one of history's most horrific villains. Hundreds of thousands died, and millions were wounded in the war to end the scourge of Hitler and his band of thugs who were killing innocent Jews, Catholics, and Gypsies. Truly civilized nations were horrified at this genocide. Now the sons of those soldiers are expected to shrug their shoulders as their teen-age daughters are told without their parents' knowledge that an abortion is the best solution to an unexpected pregnancy.

5. Many of today's fathers spend more time indulging in pornography than they do talking to their sons and daughters. I wonder how quick they would be to spend the money on this trash if they would stop to think for one minute that each and every one of those girls being exploited in those films and magazines is someone else's baby girl. Must you see your own daughter posing nude before you vote out those who fail to condemn it? What will it take before you seek legislation and police effort to end the manufacture and distribution of porn?

6. When was the last time the average 1990s dad told his kids "NO"? Today's dad wants to be "cool." He'd rather see his daughters and sons strung out on dope, dying from AIDS, or going to bed with every Tom, Jane, and Harry than disagree with the public schools' and television's promotion of licentious sex.

7. As dads plan their sons' futures, most will undoubtedly hope an excellent career, lots of money, super grandkids,

and achievement are in the stars. Does today's modern dad also hope that his son will pass along various sexually transmitted diseases to countless girlfriends? Is he looking forward to the day when he is told his son has impregnated one or two young women who then abort one or more grandkids? Is a "cool" dad hoping his son will become a homosexual? If not, how can these dads stand by while schools teach that sex outside of marriage and homosexuality are acceptable lifestyle choices?

The war is destroying our women and our sons, and it's happening while the male leadership watch "Monday Night Football." Why, oh why, have we failed to stand up for our families? What has happened to our men? If you've been waiting for leadership, there *are* men in our culture who have signaled the call to arms, many of whom are named throughout this book. They and I earnestly call upon each and every man who has ever fathered a child or who intends to father a child in the future to take the following actions:

Establish a clear-cut value system for your children. It is time to end the experiment in relative values. It is highly destructive for children and society to believe that each of us can decide what is right or wrong on the basis of what makes us feel good. The following list of core values is by no means a complete list of basic moral dictates, but it includes those which would provide your children with the healthiest and happiest future.

First a general list of values to teach your children:

• The Ten Commandments—Over 80 percent of the U.S. population who say they are Christian or Jewish honor this list found in Exodus 20:3-17.

• Christ's "greatest commandments" to "Love the Lord your God with all your heart and with all your soul and with all your mind" and to "Love your neighbor as yourself" (Matt. 22:37-39, NIV).

• The Pledge of Allegiance—Say it to yourself and think carefully about the words.

• The Boy Scout Oath—"On my honor I will do my best to do my duty to God and my country and to obey the Scout Law; to help other people at all times; to keep myself physically strong, mentally awake and morally straight." The Scout

Law—"A scout is trustworthy, loyal, helpful, friendly, courteous, kind, obedient, cheerful, thrifty, brave, clean, and reverent."

• The Optimists Creed—"Promise yourself to be so strong that nothing can disturb your peace of mind, to talk health, happiness, and prosperity to every person you meet; to make all your friends feel that there is something in them; to look at the sunnyside of everything and make your optimism come true; to think only of the best, to work only for the best, and to expect only the best; to be just as enthusiastic about the success of others as you are about your own; to forget the mistakes of the past and press onward to the greater achievements of the future; to wear a cheerful countenance at all times and give every living creature you meet a smile; to give so much time to the improvement of yourself that you have no time to criticize others; to be too large for worry, too noble for anger, too strong for fear, and too happy to permit the presence of trouble."

Now some specific areas having to do with the sexual aspect of life: (1) Sexual intercourse outside of a lifetime commitment, sealed by a public profession in marriage, is always wrong. (2) For our young women, if you are about to become a single mom, first, if possible, marry the father; second, keep the baby; and, as a last resort, give it up for adoption. Abortion is never an option. (3) For our young men, if you impregnate your girlfriend, do the honorable thing and marry her. If this is not possible, take full responsibility for the child, including financial, emotional, and spiritual support for the baby's entire life. (4) Ladies, dress discreetly. Be prepared to say no to any sexual advance beyond a kiss. (5) The use of mind-altering chemicals, including drugs and alcohol, serves no benefit. Certainly, it is always wrong to drink alcohol to excess. (6) The first evidence of civilization is mutual respect among members of that civilization, an idea commonly referred to by historians as a social contract. Each of us has a duty to repay our various communities for the life that they have provided us. This duty is a part of the social contract. If each of us were to only take and never give, all of us would have far less of everything that life has to offer. (7) Work is an invaluable component of life, providing a sense of purpose, self-worth, self-realization, and income. Whether we work as ditch diggers, trash haulers, doctors, businessmen, or housewives, we should give it all we've got. Not because we owe it to our employer (although we do), but because we will feel more joy in our labor.

You may have other values you wish to pass on to your children, resources other than those shown that present your philosophy in a different way. The key ingredient is to clearly teach a system of values that are seen to be as unchanging and unchangeable as the law of gravity. You and I and our children will be far better adjusted if we believe that our values are timeless in history and will continue to be constant for all time. Imagine how life would be if we couldn't count on gravity or the sun's daily crossing. The tumultuous result is the same if we can't count on our fellow man to behave by the values above.

Live the value system you teach. These principles are better caught than taught. Your children will be far more likely to evidence these in their lives if you are living them in yours. If you smoke, drink, swear, watch movies that include heavy sexual content, or don't treat your kids or others with respect, it will do very little good to tell your kids how they should act.

If you are having an extramarital affair, how can you tell your fifteen-year-old daughter or seventeen-year-old son sex outside of marriage isn't OK for them? If you are physically or emotionally abusive toward your kids or your wife, how can you explain the value of respect for others? If you support, work for, or vote in favor of candidates who promote abortion on demand; total freedom of expression for TV, records, and movies; recognition of homosexuality as an acceptable alternative lifestyle; and the distribution of condoms to our little girls, don't be surprised when your precious babies end up having abortions, being sexually active, or trying sex with someone of their own gender.

Monitor and direct your children's activities. From the time a child is old enough to recognize that there is a difference between him and you, he will look to you for direction. Even as a three-year-old throws a tantrum to get out of doing what you ask him, he is begging you to establish and maintain those boundaries.

In the case of the adolescent, there is only a difference of type, not kind. Even the most rebellious youngster is hoping you will provide him with rules of conduct and the backbone to enforce them.

There is an exception or two to this claim. If the rules are not backed by an authority, or if the authority is not respected, then the child will be even more likely to break them in utter defiance. If the basis for your rules are the values listed above, and if it is clear to your kids that your reasons for imposing these limits are based on your love for them and your desire that they should live long and prosper, then they are very likely to obey you a great majority of the time.

You can further increase the likelihood of your teen-agers' willing compliance if each limitation or responsibility is discussed and agreed upon. In situations where there is disagreement, at least they will know that they have had their say. In addition, discipline for failure to obey should be meted out with love and forgiveness.

Dad, here are some of the Kirk family rules. You may wish to be even more restrictive.

Dating

No dating before fifteen-and-a-half. Then, only double dates and chaperoned activities until 16. After age sixteen, evaluate the situation on a case by case basis with the following ideas in mind. (1) Girls must introduce any new boy-friend to the parents prior to the first date. (2) Strict curfews are in effect. This prevents time before and after the planned activity for parking, etc. (3) Phone calls are expected if the plan is not being followed exactly. (4) Dates cannot involve activities that contain sexually exciting material. This would include certain movies and concerts. Yes, your kids will say, "Gee, you act like you don't trust me." Your answer might go something like this: "We do trust your basic judgment. We believe that you want to do the right thing. However, it has been our experience that even the best of us can be overcome by temptation. Therefore, it is our hope that we can remove temptation from your path through these rules.

You'll have your opportunity soon enough to make all your own rules. Hopefully, you will use our example to create disciplines in your own life that will keep you from even coming near temptation." You might even tell them the following parable. I would love to credit the source, but I can't recall it. A certain man walked home from work every day along the same road. On this street was a magazine stand that sold pornographic material. Each day that he passed this stand, he found his head being turned more and more until he began to stop, just out of curiosity. Soon he found that he wanted to spend more time fulfilling his curiosity, so he bought a magazine. It wasn't long before his collection of magazines began to trouble him, and he asked a friend for advice: "What can I do to end my interest in this material?" His friend pondered the issue for a while, and then responded, "Go home by another street."

Make-up

No make-up prior to age sixteen, except for a light base if she has complexion problems. After sixteen, light-colored lipstick, a touch of blush, and mascara only are permitted during the day. Eye liner and darker lipstick are OK for evening functions. All should be in good taste, never gaudy or used as a statement of defiance. Once again, there is likely to be disagreement on this issue. The following approach has worked well for many generations of fathers. "You are at the peak of your beauty. Young men appreciate your natural beauty far more than if you cover it up with paint. Accents to bring out your best features and cover-ups to hide your minor flaws will create the best possible you." (Be sure to detail her best features glowingly, and gently, cautiously discuss how to minimize her lesser points.) You may even want to impress upon her your special knowledge of what is beautiful in a woman by reason of your being a man. Without bragging, you have really good taste (for instance, your wife), and you have a pretty good idea of what a man likes in a woman. For the final impact, remind her that the boys who are most likely to appreciate the heavy make-up are the very ones who are most likely to treat her poorly and want her only for sex.

TV, Movies, Reading Materials and Records

You will be the judge of what they see and listen to. They are to avoid all materials that are sexually explicit or provide messages that run counter to the values listed above. To a certain extent this has to be done on the honor system. It is reasonably easy to monitor movies. You may want to see any PG-13 or R rated movies that are of interest to your kids before allowing them to go. You could also ask friends you trust for their review. There are even two services that describe in detail those elements of a film that may not fit your value system. One is called Preview Movie Morality Guide (call 1-214-231-9910 for information). The other is Movie Guide (1-800-899-MOVIE). The objection to your censorship of these materials may be the most strident of all. Once again, I would use the argument about trusting their judgment, but not wanting to create tempting situations more than necessary. We may trust their balance, also, but we would not approve of their doing a tightrope act at twenty stories without a net. TV is somewhat more difficult. As I write this, it is almost Christmas. Last night, while watching the Hollywood Christmas Parade on TV, one actress told all my kids and yours as well, that she was going to spend her weekend making love with her boyfriend. My ten-year-old daughter looked over her shoulder at me and just sighed. As a bare minimum, make certain programs off limits. My kids may not watch a music video on any channel, and MTV is OUT. Those programs who make sex the central theme are obviously out. Many basically excellent shows have now decided they have to add their two cents worth concerning the acceptability of premarital and extramarital sex, homosexual love, and abortion. Once anyone in our family sees that a series has pushed any portion of this agenda, that show is no longer available in our household. I can't be sure that your kids will react the same, but mine agree. There isn't even any fighting about it. The reasons are simple enough. Why would any of us want to be preached to on subjects which could, were we to follow the teaching, disrupt, damage, or even end our lives?

Books, Magazines, and Radio

It is almost impossible to keep a child who really wants to see and hear filth from getting hold of it. In this situation, I can only propose that you tell your kids how you feel about it. Explain in detail how it can harm them. Explain how it can be even more dangerous to their health and well-being than drugs. Be sure they understand that you will be very disappointed if they seek out and use this material in spite of your feelings. Ask them if they agree with you. If they don't, continue the dialogue so that all points of view can be discussed. You want them to see the validity of your argument, even if they aren't totally convinced it is the best approach.

Provide an appropriate environment for your kids. When a farmer wants to grow strong, healthy plants, he seeks fertile soil and plenty of sunshine. He then shelters the new seedlings from the cold, weeds, insects, and other elements which might damage or destroy his crop before it reaches maturity. He also provides nourishment and proper care to insure each plant its maximum opportunity to produce its yield.

Your job as a dad is much the same. We have already touched on your responsibility with regard to providing for the physical and emotional needs of your children. We have discussed some of the aspects of care and protection that you must undertake if you are to have success in child-rearing. Let's now take a moment to discuss the fertile soil and the sunshine.

Four things most influence today's youth: parents, television, school, and peers. Each and every one of these environmental aspects will seriously impact your child's growth and eventual character. You have a reasonable chance of success in being able to determine whether the parental (you and your wife's) influence will be positive or negative, since you are half of that unit. There are a number of resources, some noted in the bibliography, that provide guidance in establishing a healthy media environment. What's left? How can you maximize your influence on peers and school?

Peers

You should be fully engaged in the determination of whom your children hang out with. If they run with other youth who are involved in drugs, sex, shoplifting, ditching school, or other negative behavior, they will undoubtedly follow along. What steps might you take if one of your youngsters is already associating with the wrong crowd?

1. Address the situation with your child. Without talking about his (or her) friends just yet, explain your values once again in such a way that the discussion can be applied to his friends later in the conversation. Allow him to respond with any disagreements he may have about your values. You may learn quite a lot from such an open forum.

Once you have softened him up, and he is beginning to think about how he may have gotten a bit off the track, ask if he thinks that his current group of friends would agree with the values you've just outlined. Ask him to judge the likely outcome for his associates if they continue along the path they are currently walking. Ask him if this is what he wants for his life. Generally, you won't have to say very much more. Most kids have relationships with more than one group. In many cases you may see a dramatic shift in associations after one or a few such eyeball-to-eyeball discussions.

2. Many parents will make the mistake of forbidding their child to continue a friendship with certain individuals. Kids see this as an invasion of their basic rights and will fight any such intrusion tooth and nail. If the first approach doesn't work, you must create the separation without any indication that the associates are the problem.

This separation can be accomplished by asking the school to change your child's class, or to make certain that they are not in the same class at the beginning of the next term. You might also try enrolling your youngster in after-school activities that provide opportunities to form friendships, such as sports, art or music classes, Scouts (including Explorers), community service, or drama.

Increase his work load at home in order to reduce the opportunity to hang out. Restrict phone calls to five minutes on school nights and fifteen minutes on weekends. Discourage forms of amusement that are likely to include the bad seeds; malls, arcades, and homes where parents aren't present provide breeding grounds for trouble. We have a very strict rule against even an eighteen-year-old having a friend over when we're not home.

If you still can't break the bonds, move him to another school. In some school districts you will be able to merely select a different school within the public school system. This may mean you have to do some driving, but this very minor sacrifice should not deter you. You may need to make a much bigger sacrifice and enroll him in a private school. This will have the additional benefit of improving his education as well. If you are still unsuccessful, the sacrifice may get steeper. However, I know personally of two families who have taken the bold tactic of moving the child completely out of the area of temptation. In both cases, the youngster was the only one moved. In one case, a budding gang member was sent to his grandparents in Central America in preference to central Los Angeles. In a second case, the grandparents were only twenty miles down the freeway.

If there are no willing relatives to help out, you may need to move the entire family. It goes without saying that this would be expensive and disruptive. However, if someone was standing in front of your kid with a pistol pointed at his face, threatening to blow out his brains, wouldn't you be willing to do whatever was prudent and necessary to save his life? In many scenarios, your child is faced with this very prospect if he remains tied to his current companions.

3. You may be able to accomplish the goal of separating your child from an unhealthy peer group and much more by becoming active in a church or synagogue. He will have a new set of acquaintances from which to choose friends. Most churches have many youth activities which will redirect his attention. The values that are taught will conflict with the values held by his other group, and he will have to choose. Your own participation will be an excellent witness of your concern for the values you have preached.

4. Any time along this process you may want to try counseling. If you attend a church, you may want to begin with a visit to the pastor or other spiritual leader of the

church. In many cases, he will be able to provide all the help you need to rebuild relationships with your child and change his behavior patterns. If the church leader feels that he would not be able to handle the situation, or you are not finding what you need through this resource, he may be able to suggest outside counseling that will coincide with your beliefs.

If you are not a member of a church, you might ask friends for recommendations. If you do not have the funds for private counseling, many social agencies offer free or reduced-fee help. Check with your city or county department of social services. (Be especially careful when using these agencies, that the counselor agrees with your values.) Once you have selected a counselor, make it clear what you hope to accomplish. In some cases you may be most interested in arresting certain attitudes and behaviors. In other situations you may feel it is most important to work on the child's self-esteem or image. Commonly, the problem is entirely one of association, and no amount of counseling is likely to convince your teen to give up his friends.

5. Numerous studies have concluded that the number one predictor of whether a child's behavior becomes antisocial or rebellious is that child's relationship with his parents. Following the above approaches will definitely result in your spending quality time with your child. The mere evidence that you care enough to become active in your teenager's life may be the only thing needed to turn his or her life around.

School

Even the best public schools are a travesty today. The clear proof of this is that a very large percentage of public school teachers and administrators send their own kids to private schools. If that doesn't say enough, I challenge you to spend a day at school with one of your kids.

Regardless of what you perceive to be the cause of the problems in public education, there is unfortunately an even greater cancer eating away at our schools. The standards of moral conduct that form the underpinning of a just civilization are no longer taught in our public schools. The very list presented at the beginning of this chapter has been removed from the textbooks of the schools we pay for with our tax dollars. Our kids now sit at the knee of teachers who teach the gospel of moral relativism and dispel any notion that there might be absolute standards of morality or character.

I know that many of you don't think you can afford private school. I wouldn't have my kids in a public school if it cost me my last penny. There are many excellent, private, religious schools which charge only two to three hundred dollars per month. You can school your children at home and give them an incredible education and a great relationship with you for only about a thousand dollars per year.

If you still don't think it would be worth the sacrifice, read your kids' social studies books and see if you can find the clear moral teachings of our forefathers, the importance of religion in the settlement of America, or the contributions of Western civilization to our current world of peace. In place of these cultural building blocks you will find attacks on democracy, Columbus, capitalism, and business. If you still have a social studies book from the fifties or before, compare the two and see how history has been rewritten to fit the popular philosophies of today.

Sex

It may seem as though we have been far afield from the primary subject matter of this book. However, every issue above relates directly to your son's or daughter's likelihood of being physically or emotionally injured or even killed by sex. If they are in tune with your value system, acknowledge your rules and restrictions on their behavior, and live in an environment where positive influences are paramount, they will be far less likely to engage in illicit sex.

I challenge each and every reader to come up with any other behavior, activity, or aspect of life which is filled with more danger. I further challenge you to find any other aspect of our culture that is negatively affecting a larger percentage of our population. We spend millions of dollars on cancer, heart disease, and AIDS. No single disease has close to the number of victims as illicit sex.

Our schools and media work overtime to help convince our youngsters to stay away from smoking, alcohol, and drugs, but together these stalkers don't ruin as many young lives as do the consequences of teen sex. We have armies of government employees working to reduce air pollution, job-related injuries, deaths and injuries due to auto accidents, and illnesses caused by poorly prepared or packaged foods. However, the death toll from abortions alone (1.5 million babies per year) eclipses all deaths from any other cause, and what is the government doing to help prevent abortions? They're handing out condoms. What thinking person believes this is going to work? (No report to date has shown anything but an increase in pregnancies due to free condom programs.)

I think it will be up to you, Dad, to make the difference in your kids' lives. You aren't going to be able to turn the job over to the schools. They've already botched it. You surely don't want any other branch of government dealing in such a private matter. Your kids' friends and the TV are definitely going to impede, not help, your efforts. And unfortunately, most churches are doing very little to help.

Nope, I think it will be up to you, Dad, to explain the birds and bees, teach appropriate values, monitor and direct behavior, and provide the love and support each of your children will need to get through these years without a sexual disaster. For many of you, this could be one of the toughest things you've ever done. It isn't easy to sit down with a youngster and discuss something as intimate as sex. It isn't made any easier by the fact that the words and the parts of the anatomy are normally taboo. But consider the consequences if you don't forget your inhibitions and do your job—a ruined life, disease, even death.

It is my hope that the next section of this chapter will provide you with a general method of bringing this topic to your children that will help both you and them enjoy the process rather than dread it.

The Key to Virginity

Pam's first-born, the little baby with the big, hazel eyes, recently turned sixteen. She is my adopted daughter (as is her sister), and I am proud to say that no natural father ever cared more for his kids than I do these two.

For her sixteenth birthday, Pam and I took Christian out

to a very special dinner, one which Pam and I had planned over many months. The subject of the dinner was our love and concern for her and our interest in helping her to have a clear understanding of her sexuality.

I am indebted for the idea for this dinner and the material that follows to a pastor and his wife in southern California by the names of Richard C. and Reneé Durfield. They have written a wonderful book, entitled *Raising Them Chaste*. Rather than paraphrase their work, let me tell you about the wonderful experience that Pam, Christian, and I shared that evening.

Christian knew the evening was to be special. She was provided money to purchase a special dress for the dinner. She had her hair, nails, and all the fixings done. We were very proud parents when she walked in the room looking like Cinderella going to the ball.

We headed to one of the fanciest eateries in our part of town, and as we sat down, Christian's already wide eyes were round with anticipation. We said grace over the meal and talked about the things teen-agers care about as we enjoyed the appetizers and main course. After the dishes were cleared away, we told her of our mission. We said that we wanted to discuss her sexuality.

First, we wanted to be certain that she had a clear understanding of the basics—that if she had any questions, we wanted to answer them that night. In addition, there were some new things we wanted to present to her. She proposed that we go first.

Pam and I talked about many of the things contained elsewhere in this book: about the sexual nature of boys and how they differ from girls; about the lines that many boys might use and how she could combat these; about the importance of abstinence and how glad we were that she felt strongly about waiting for lovemaking until marriage. She posed her questions all along the way. Were all boys that way? No, but it was better to expect such behavior and be glad when it didn't come. How far do you think a couple can go without getting carried away? Chaste (mouth closed) kissing, hand-holding, hugging—anything more strikes the match. After we had exhausted the ideas we came to discuss and

answered any and all questions she asked, we brought out
her gift. She was clearly moved by the special ring we had
made for the occasion. We had some old rings melted down,
and by using the old gold and one of the diamonds, a jeweler
made us a ring in the shape of a key. Inset into the heart-
shaped head of the key was a solitaire diamond. The shaft of
the old-fashioned key wrapped around her finger and came
back to meet the heart.

We explained to her that this key was the key to her
heart and to her virginity. She was to wear it at all times as
a reminder of a vow we wanted her to make with God that
she would give this gift to her husband on her wedding day.
It would also cause any young man who dated her to become
informed of her decision, since he would have to be pretty
obtuse not to notice and ask about this unusual ring.

Christian readily agreed to this plan. I said that I wanted
each of us to pray about what we had experienced that
evening, and this time she asked to go first. Pastor Durfield
feels that it is important that the young person be willing to
pray in a public place without shame. This is evidence that
they are not going to be intimidated by the world around
them when deciding to do the right thing.

I can't recommend enough that you, or you and your
wife, take each of your children to such a dinner. That
evening was one of the most precious and memorable I have
spent in my life. For some you may wish to do it at an earlier
age. You'll have to judge your children's maturity and needs.
You may wish to purchase a necklace, bracelet, or other
piece of jewelry that embodies the key symbolism. By giving
this gift and spending this evening together, you will instill
in them a clear understanding of your feelings on the issue
of premarital sex. Through the strong emphasis of this statement you will gain the best possible chance of giving your
daughter away as a virgin.

In addition to your responsibility to teach your children
how to handle their sexuality in a responsible manner, you
also need to be in the business of protecting them from
those who would work against your effort. Your first effort
should be directed at the school your children attend. I

would suggest you begin with a letter to the principal and the school board as follows:

Dear Principal and School Board Members:

My child, Susy Smith, is enrolled in the 7th grade of George Washington Middle School. Because of values that we hold dear, we insist that:

1. Our daughter not be included in any sex education class where the following elements are present:

A. Co-educational discussion of sexual topics;

B. Any method other than abstinence discussed as an acceptable method of birth control except in marriage;

C. Presentation of premarital or extramarital sex as acceptable or a matter of choice for each person;

D. Homosexuality, incest, pedophilia, bestiality, group or any other type of sexual deviancy presented as a lifestyle choice;

E. Detailed descriptions of or promotion of "outersex" (petting, mutual masturbation, oral or anal sex) as an acceptable practice for those who aren't married.

2. Our daughter never be given, sold, or counseled to purchase any type of birth control product or device.

3. Our daughter never be counseled to obtain an abortion or to withhold information from her mother and I about any aspect of her health or well-being.

We recognize that you have the right to tell her that she may legally withhold certain information. We specifically withhold any right you may think you have to recommend abortion or the withholding of the aforementioned information as a positive course of action.

You may wish to circulate copies of this letter to any members of the faculty or staff who may be in a position to subvert our wishes. We fully intend to proceed with appropriate legal action against any individual, group, or entity that in any way acts against our express wishes as stated herein.

> Sincerely,
>
> Bob and Jane Smith

Next, I would send the following letter to Planned Parenthood, to any and all abortion counseling centers or abortion clinics in your area, and to your family doctor.

Dr. Jones:

> We are the parents of Susy Smith. We recognize that as the law now stands, our daughter may come to you without our knowledge or permission and ask that an abortion be performed to destroy the baby she may someday create.
>
> We, however, believe that the law does not give you an unrestricted right to advise her to have an abortion or to advise her against seeking our counsel. Therefore, if at any time during her minority, Susy Smith comes to you to seek advice as to what she should do about a crisis pregnancy, we specifically forbid you from advising or influencing her in any way toward an abortion or against seeking our counsel prior to that abortion.
>
> It is our position that you may provide her with balanced materials or arguments with regard to the pros and cons of keeping the baby, offering it for adoption, or aborting. However, as a part of those materials or discussion, she must be informed of the potential for physical, mental, emotional, and spiritual trauma resulting from abortion. You must also point out to her that the child she is carrying is "alive."
>
> In that your organization has either a monetary advantage or a philosophical predisposition to abortion as the best method for handling a crisis pregnancy, we believe that your disregard for our rights as listed above which results in an abortion and/or any harm to our daughter would be actionable in a court of law.
>
> Sincerely,
>
> Bob and Jane Smith

You and Your Son

Please be certain to read the chapter on mothers and also the one for teen-age boys; you will be able to pick up substantial ideas from these chapters as to specific approaches you might use with your boys. In the chapter for mothers, I put a great deal of the burden on her shoulders of teaching your son about how he should behave. I did this for a number of reasons. First, moms commonly find it easier to talk about this subject than dads do. Second, dads sometimes are unwilling to tell their sons to absolutely abstain. Third, in today's world, it is too common for dads to be out of the picture. Fourth, it is far more likely that mom will bring a spiritual/moral context to the discussion.

However, it is my sincere hope that you will talk to your son and clearly admonish him to remain chaste until marriage. I won't repeat the reasons previously outlined in other chapters why he should do so. But if you are willing to have that discussion, your words will have a much more profound effect on him than those of anyone else who might so instruct him. Please remember that his friends, school, TV, radio, records, movies, newspapers, popular books, and teen magazines are all telling him that it is either all right to have sex outside of marriage or that abstinence just isn't reality. If his mother is the only person in the whole world who disagrees, it's still pretty tough for him to make the right choice.

In addition to giving him sound advice about abstinence, I would recommend that you speak to him in depth on two issues. (Mom, if dad won't or can't address these, please try to get a clear understanding of these two subjects and help your son with them.) Beyond the potential danger lurking in premarital sexual activity today, the next two most likely sexual problems your son will face are pornography and homosexuality.

Pornography, the Progressive Disease

Most men who read this next section will know it is the truth. The very few who have not experienced it might still recognize some of the tugs in their own life from this insidious creature. Women are hard-pressed to understand it at

all, but there seems to be a growing recognition among
women that pornography is a great deal more than a harm-
less diversion.

The presentation that follows is possibly one of the most
telling descriptions in print of how the progressive nature of
pornography becomes addictive to the user. I have inten-
tionally written this as tastefully as possible; I am not interested in either offending or titillating the reader, but rather
informing and preparing fathers and mothers in this matter.
Most men who are addicted to porn would rather admit to
an affair than to how important this material is to them.

I am highly qualified to write about the effects of porn;
I have plenty of personal experience in my past as a user. I
also have the experience of having a loving wife tell me in
no uncertain terms to put it aside. It was one of the nicest
things she ever said to me.

This section is also intended as a signal to adult male
users of pornographic materials to put it out of their lives.
I also encourage wives who know their husbands are in
trouble with porn to help them get it behind them.

It all starts with man's curiosity and his natural enjoyment in visual stimulation. A young boy or man may start his
interest in erotic material with something as simple as adver-
tisements for ladies' undergarments or pictures of bare-
breasted natives in *National Geographic*. (I've often wondered
how much of their readership *National Geographic* would lose
if they stopped exploiting teen-age native girls. I doubt
whether they can make a great case for the educational value
of these pictures.)

When a male is exposed to such material, he is sexually
excited by it. Whether or not he relieves the sexual tension
created by such material, the excitement is nevertheless part
of the interest.

However, like drug or alcohol addiction, whatever the
first stimulus, it fails to excite at some point. The voyeur now
hopes to find a bra ad that has not been airbrushed. The
National Geographic reader hopes for bigger busts or younger
girls or different angles. But soon this isn't enough either.
The mainline magazines such as *Playboy* and *Penthouse* may
fill the bill for quite a while longer. Even here the newly

addicted will tear open the latest edition looking for something he hasn't seen before. It always has to be something new.

Then these magazines aren't enough—they have their own limits. So now he graduates to other legal magazines which show simulated or actual sexual activity in every pose, with every sex toy, and deviance galore. As the material becomes more and more degrading of the human condition, the requirement for something more deviant accelerates. "Art" movie theaters, home videos, and bookstore peep shows are the next to last stop in the two-dimensional range of materials. These legal materials include sadism, masochism, and use of excrement.

In the meantime, live shows may become part of the picture. Topless, bottomless, live sex, and more can be found in almost any major city either openly and legally, or in the more expensive underground.

The final stop is illegal material, which would include use of children, animals, and torture/murder in the themes. Your son may not use pornography at all. Or it may be that he reached the *Playboy* or *Hustler* stage and that was enough for him. Like a social drinker, he may really like those magazines, but he doesn't need to get drunk every night.

Or you may be shocked to find out just how far gone one of your loved ones is. You see, there are mountains of this stuff sold. *Somebody's* buying it.

Dad, where are you in this cycle? Do you feel yourself being pulled into destruction? Where can it lead? What are the consequences?

In the most extreme cases, it can lead to many types of deviant behavior. According to the President's Commission Report on Pornography, there is a clear connection between the use of these materials and criminal sexual behavior such as rape, child molestation, and even brutal beatings, torture, and murder. The consequences for the average home are less horrible, but very serious indeed.

Adult men commonly must fantasize about this material to become excited when having relations with their own wives. This is not because their wives are no longer exciting, but because the pornography offers things they can't. Clearly this will increase the likelihood of husbands looking for additional excitement outside the marriage.

Many men will find self-stimulation through porn to be far more gratifying and easier than having intercourse with their wives. This may decrease the frequency of their relations, setting up a situation in which either one or both may feel the need to look elsewhere for sexual release.

Recent studies have indicated that men who have used pornography to masturbate are having difficulties in their marital relations. The two-dimensional lovers of their youth never talked back, never had a headache, and were always incredibly beautiful and perfectly made-up. They were also willing to do things which the husband is now unwilling to ask his wife to do, or which she feels uncomfortable doing.

When porn is in the house, it will eventually be seen by the children; it can never be hidden well enough. When a twelve-year-old boy finds his dad's stash, it isn't too difficult to imagine the results of his becoming desensitized to a wide variety of sexual excesses so early in his life. Of course, your son may not need to find your stash. Any one of his friends may have access to his dad's library. In some cases, the friend's dad may have no problem at all with his son's enjoyment of this material.

High on the list of consequences comes that word again: respect. How can a man who sees women in all these poses, doing all these unimaginable things, so clearly enjoying all of it, and so willingly allowing men to hurt them—how can this man move into the real world without a reduced respect for, or wrong ideas about, all women? How can he enter into a relationship with a flesh and blood woman and not take the lessons he's learned from porn into that relationship?

Therefore, I implore the wives who are reading this: If you know that your husband is into this, ask him to stop. Tell him that it is offensive to you that he needs something more than you to satisfy his needs. Tell him that you don't wish to compete with photographs, film, and video tape. Tell him you don't want your kids to find the stuff. Let him know it's really important to you that he get rid of it. He will thank you later (maybe never, verbally, but in his heart).

Homosexuality—It Isn't an Acceptable Alternative Lifestyle

One of the best remembered aspects of George Orwell's *1984* is the concept of newspeak. Much of what he predicted for our nation was far off the mark. Democracy was and still is alive and well. However, if there is evidence that Orwell could see into the future, it has been in the campaign of misinformation generated by those in the homosexual movement. In just over one generation they have been able to manipulate our thinking through every imaginable form of misstatement, lie, distortion, and fraud.

A large part of our population is said to believe that homosexuality is like being left-handed or near-sighted. The homosexual cannot decide for himself, they say, and society should not try to change his orientation.

These are the same folks who tell us that being "gay" is a lifestyle choice, and we all know that Americans are for choice. If they choose to engage in homosexual acts or to lead a "gay" lifestyle, they should have the right to do so. They also tell us that gays are a minority group like blacks or women. They need and deserve special protection under the law in order to avoid discrimination by the public at large, especially homophobes.

Please consider this closely: The homosexual community, doctors and other scientists engaged in research on the subject, and the assorted psychologists and psychoanalysts who work with homosexuals can't agree as to whether homosexuality is inherited, the result of environment, a lifestyle choice, or all of the above some of the time. And the answer has nothing to do with the correct way to deal with the issue.

If your child is confused about his sexuality, or if he has already engaged in homosexual acts, or believes that he is homosexual, you need to act fast. Whatever the origin, homosexuals have been "going straight" for decades under caring counsel and are doing so today by the thousands.

The gay rights people have taken poll after poll to prove that homosexuals are well-adjusted and are happy with their "choice" or "lot in life," depending on what they are trying to prove. I have never met a parent in my life who hopes his child becomes a homosexual. I have never met a heterosexual who hoped he himself would change and become "gay." This would certainly seem to suggest that those who have come in contact with homosexuals have not perceived them to have an equal or better lot in life.

Numerous studies have indicated that homosexuals are far more likely to be promiscuous than the "straight" population. In addition, other evidence would suggest they have a much greater likelihood of sexual interest in young children. There is even an organization large enough to support paid staff and a magazine promoting lowering the age of consent so that they can indulge their interest in young people.

It doesn't take a scientific study to prove that the most extreme elements of this community are seriously disturbed. They demonstrate this openly in public through their extremely outrageous behavior.

New information indicates that homosexuals have a life expectancy of only forty-two years. That is before AIDS is factored in. Taking AIDS into consideration lowers life expectancy to thirty-nine.

There is an insistence upon continuing the lie that 10 percent of the population is homosexual. This figure has been shown to be an outright fabrication and a lie from its earliest inception. However, through the continuous bombardment of the public with this outright fiction, the fiction has taken on the aura of fact. It is important to the gay rights agenda that this number be accepted. It would be so much harder to demand special attention or prove the normality of this unfortunate lifestyle if the real number of 2 percent or less was generally known and believed.

If you have any question about the percentage, the Center for Disease Control, a U.S. government agency, is one formidable group who has arrived at the 2 percent number. However, ask yourself, of the few hundred people that you know well enough to make a guess, how many would you say are, or even could be, homosexual? You'll soon discover that ten out of one hundred is ludicrous and that two out of one hundred seems a little high.

As a father of a young man or daughter whom you certainly hope and pray will have a normal sex life, be aware of some reality in the face of constant newspeak from the press.

I want to dispel some myths about early signs. Minor behaviors in children that are normally associated with the opposite sex don't mean anything in this context. If your little boy likes to play with neighborhood girls, even prefers them to boys, this alone is not an indication of problems. Don't discourage his interest in dolls, girls, or playing house. Being interested or good in sports doesn't have anything to do with sexual orientation. If your daughter is a tomboy, it doesn't mean she'll grow up a lesbian. Sensitivity in boys or the lack of it in girls is not much of a clue either. It may have far more to do with which hemisphere of the brain is dominant.

Put two or three of these together, and you may have more to be concerned about. If your ten-year-old boy is still playing with dolls instead of baseballs, you should get an outside opinion. If you never see a twelve-year-old boy show any interest in girls because they are girls, the drama increases. Perfectly normal boys may not show any social interest in girls until high school; however, almost all boys will be interested in the anatomy, whether or not they are interested in the brain.

If you have serious doubts about your teen-age or older boy, don't kid him, give him a hard time, or tiptoe around it. Ask him. "Son, I need to have a heart-to-heart talk with you. It can sometimes be very confusing to be a teen-ager. One of the most confusing parts is the sexual thing. You and I have talked about the birds and the bees and all that. However, I sense that maybe there are questions on your mind right now that you're having a hard time bringing up to me. Is that so?" If he says yes, let him know you really care about his questions and ask him to please trust you with them. If this leads nowhere, you might go on, "An interesting thing about the sexual side of our lives is that sometimes we think we're weird. You know, everybody else does something, and we don't. Or we do something, and nobody else is like that. Do you sometimes have those kinds of feelings?" If he says yes, tell him that you remember having those kinds of feelings. Maybe give him an example. Then ask for one of his.

If you're still not making any progress, you may want to

tell him, "I can also remember worrying about whether I was a 100 percent all-American man. All kinds of ideas went through my mind. I mean, my friends called me queer often enough (of course, I guess I called them some names, too); it just made me think about it. Do you ever worry or think about that part of your sexuality?" If he says yes or no, gently probe. You see, if he said no, he is not telling all the truth because all boys have these thoughts. Either way, you are still a long way from finding out what you need to know.

The most telling question you would really like to get to is, "Well son, when you get sexually excited, is it from seeing or thinking about girls? Have you ever become aroused from thinking about boys?" Once again, if the answers you get cause you to honestly believe there is a possibility of actual homosexual behavior or of confused gender identification, get your son to a therapist. (A caution against some of those in the counseling business: Ask the counselor if he believes homosexuality is curable and should be treated. About 25 percent think it is an acceptable lifestyle. Stay away from these.)

If the problem is with your daughter, turn this job over to your wife. The questioning could proceed along the same pathways. However, as with all things female, the feelings will be more important than the physical manifestations.

Conclusion

Dad, talk to your kids about their attitudes. Stay in touch with them about their values. Teach them and model the values you want them to take with them when they go out on their own. Be prepared to discuss their sexuality openly and honestly. Be an available source for their concerns, questions, and experiences.

Love them and provide the security of the kind of love that doesn't depend on their actions. Give them limits and discipline as an expression of your love and concern for them, not as an expression of your hostility or anger for their failures.

Remember when it is appropriate to be a father and when to be a friend. They have plenty of people around them who will reinforce their worst instincts and thinking.

You must be prepared to suffer a temporary loss of their affection or esteem because you wouldn't let them do what they thought they wanted to do. But also make your reasons clear, and offer plenty of room for reasoned debate and appropriate compromise.

Tough job, huh? It's really tough if you intend to do it right. The consequences of messing up this job are serious indeed, however. You don't have to look very far to find folks who will quickly tell you how their parents messed up their lives. I've already explained that I'm not quick to agree with those who fail to take responsibility for their own messes, but this much is clear: You, Dad, can and will affect your children's lives. You may work hard and do everything the best way you know how and still have some, or even a lot, of heartache. You may mess up at every turn and end up with great kids. That's how life is. For the most part, however, you have a big hand in chiseling the emotional and spiritual life of that child. It is a grave responsibility. How are you doing so far?

Be certain to read all of the other chapters in this book. The balance of this book calls on you to lead your family in an effort to change America.

NINE

An Earnest Warning to All Men

❖

*In 1976 less than half as many fathers as in 1957 said that
providing for children was a life goal. . . . Fewer than half of all
adult Americans today regard the idea of sacrifice for others as a
positive moral virtue.*

> Barbara Dafoe Whitehead,
> "Dan Quayle Was Right"
> *Atlantic Monthly*, April 1993

If a foreign army was poised on our borders ready to
attack our cities, destroy our freedoms, impose their culture,
rape our women, and pillage our possessions, would you be
willing to take up arms and defend your country and family?
I honestly believe that almost every man reading this book
would be headed out the door to the closest induction center the minute there was any such threat.

If Iraq or China were to begin a massive arms build-up
and mobilization intended to attack and occupy the home-
lands of our major allies, would you be ready to help in the
effort to hold back such a plan? Would you be willing to
fight and encourage your sons to fight? Again, I believe you
would.

Wake up! The war has already begun. The enemy troops
are well within our borders. Our cities are being attacked,
and our children are already dying by the millions. Our
freedoms are being undermined. Our culture is in shreds.

Our women are being raped daily. Our possessions are being stolen and defaced. The time has come to take up arms. The time has come to fight for what we believe and hold dear. The time has come to fight for the honor of our women. The time has come to defend our children. The time has come to stop hiding inside our homes and move to the streets to fight off the enemy who would take all we have.

At this moment we will not need bullets or tanks. We will fight the enemy with his own weapons. But make no mistake, there will be many casualties. Many will be bruised and broken. Others will surely die. If your reading of the first six chapters hasn't made this last paragraph crystal clear, allow me to add more evidence.

Our cities are being attacked by gangs of young thugs who have joined together because they have no structure in their lives. They are bereft of moral values and have no concept of loving their neighbor. The only social contract they know is that which their gang lives by. The gang and its members are the center of their lives; illegal drug trafficking, defense of turf, and a wide variety of illegal activities dominate their lives. Gang killings now take a larger toll each year than did most years of the Vietnam War. If a foreign enemy were killing, maiming, and plundering this many of our citizens, we would be threatening nuclear retaliation. What are we doing? Putting up bigger fences, stronger locks, and more sophisticated alarms and trying to move to some remote place in this once-great land that hasn't been touched yet by this scourge.

As a nation we have said we have had enough of sexual exploitation in the work place. We now have laws and programs to insure that companies monitor and control their employees' behavior when it comes to advances made to the opposite sex. How can we be so concerned about sexual harassment of adult women in the office or factory, but not put our foot down about the sexual harassment of our daughters on a date? It would seem that it is tied to economics in the work place. The idea seems to be that a woman is under a different kind of pressure when her job or career is at stake. The pressure is different, but the result is the same. And our little girls are far less able to defend themselves.

Surely, we want men to exercise appropriate behavior in the work place. In order to accomplish that, it will be necessary to once again teach the social contract of mutual respect. The invading hordes don't believe in this contract. It will take a war to change the tide of their victory.

Our possessions are being stolen at an alarming rate. Automobiles, bicycles, stereos, and tools disappear at ever increasing rates. Some would have us believe that this is due to economic conditions and that these thieves do what they do because they aren't able to make a living any other way. On closer investigation, however, it turns out that the largest percentage of these crimes are committed for drug money, not food money. In order to end the plunder of our possessions we must first end the plunder of our value system. It will be necessary to win victories that favor the traditional family, value-centered education, and serious consequences for those who violate our laws.

Considering the previous discussions on premarital sex, homosexuality, abortion, and pornography, as well as these additional arguments, the question is legitimate: Are we so spineless that we won't stand up and be counted in an effort to preserve values we hold dear?

In order for you to be effective in any war, you have to begin by living the values you intend to fight for. If you don't believe in democracy or freedom, you won't make a very good soldier in a war to preserve those principles. If you are to sign up to help fight the war against the sexual revolution, you may need to walk away from some aspects of that revolution of which you have been a part.

First, many who are reading this material are sexually active with someone who is not their wife. You surely can't be an effective warrior if you enter this fight with that handicap. Either discontinue the sexual aspect of the relationship or discontinue the relationship altogether!

Second, far more of you are using pornographic material. Some may only be buying the occasional magazine or video. Others are addicted and have dozens of magazines or tapes stashed away. Throw them out. Decide today that it would be impossible to put on the uniform for a fight against sexual deviancy while helping the profits of those who exploit young women.

Third, a small number of you are having difficulty in containing your sexual desires. You may be a practicing homosexual, have serious problems with pornography, or be involved in pedophilia, incest, or other serious sexual disorders. You must seek outside professional help. These types of disorders can be cured or at least moderated by the intervention of a caring counselor. Be certain to see a Christian counselor who will lovingly move you out of the behavior. Many secular counselors will actually try to convince you that the behavior is OK.

In addition, there are very large numbers who are enslaved by other non-sexual, harmful behaviors, which will clearly interfere with their ability to lead the charge to a better world. If you are using excessive amounts of alcohol or prescription drugs, involved with illegal drugs, spending the grocery money on gambling, or engaged in illegal activities of any sort, you will be hard-pressed to keep your mind on the battle to improve the moral climate of our nation. Your sons and daughters are more likely to learn your behavior than to learn to avoid the consequences of that behavior.

Men, we are called upon by God to be the leaders of our families and our nation. This is in no way meant to call into question a woman's role in leadership, nor a woman's ability to effectively lead others. However, both history and the Bible point clearly to the men as the primary source of leadership. It would appear, on the other hand, that American men in the 1990s have abdicated their responsibility to lead. Our men seem to be so caught up in themselves that they have no time to think about others; they take advantage of women, impregnate them or pass on a sexual disease, and then leave them. Too many commit to a lifetime of marriage, then take off at the first sign of trouble. Their drugs, beer, TV, and pornography are more important to them than their kids.

The time has come for men to reclaim their proper role in this society. However, the women of America are not going to allow that to happen if the men continue to be irresponsible. They will only be led by men who have a crystal clear notion of right and wrong, who will defend them to the death, and who are prepared to sacrifice to maintain their values.

Overcoming the negative influences in our own lives is only half the change that will need to take place if men are to regain the respect necessary to lead. There is also the requirement to represent and teach correct thought and deed. This is, of course, made substantially easier to the extent that the negative behaviors above have been abandoned. Have you considered the attributes that you would undoubtedly want your children to possess as they leave the protection of the nest you have built for them? Are you teaching these values to your kids or only hoping they'll end up like that . . . somehow? Are you living these virtues or praying that they will have more wisdom than you?

Lead a God-centered Life

Almost all of the rest will fall into place if the first can be achieved. Does this mean that if a person goes to church, he will never struggle with temptation or be a party to evil deeds or sin? Does this suggest that a person who is devout, prayerful, and faithful will never slip into behavior or thinking that would be out of God's will or commandments? The answer to both questions is the same: NO!

In the first place, going to church, by itself, is no guarantee that a person is leading a God-centered life. Those outside the church are often fond of calling those who are members of a local body of believers hypocrites. The non-church-going public is not alone in this recognition. Folks who go to church know that there are those in their midst who fall from grace regularly and others whose attendance doesn't fit at all with their lives the other six days of the week, often because their faith is nonexistent or weak.

Then there are those who, regardless of participation in an organized church, have truly dedicated their lives to God and have an abiding faith. These, too, are known to slip into sin or even to fall. The good news is that they can repent and be forgiven. The stronger their faith, and the greater their commitment to an unseen God, the more likely they are to lead a virtuous life.

I have seen this result in my own life. As a youth I was one of those who felt the church was falling short of its purpose. While my faith was strong, my interest in organized religion was zilch. For almost fifteen years I avoided the church, and believed that my faithfulness was as strong as ever. During this rebellious period, I enjoyed a great deal of what the seventies offered; I also fell prey to some elements of the humanistic teachings of the time and struggled with issues related to moral relativism. I crossed back and forth in a narrow range in my thinking about such things as abortion, the death penalty, sexual liberation, the inerrancy of the Bible, and the necessity of salvation for everlasting life in the presence of God.

During the years that I have been back in the church and have steadily increased my devotion to God, my study of His Word, and my time in His presence, I have just as steadily lost interest in those parts of my life which were dishonoring to Him. Because I was desirous of making God the center of my life, I didn't need or care about those things anymore. Furthermore, just because I have been freed from the bondage of those few sins, it doesn't mean that there isn't a great deal of work to do. The struggle goes on in other areas of my life. Many teachers have compared this process to peeling an onion. As you remove each layer, there is another below. The next layer may be smaller, fresher, and more supple, but it too must be removed before you can get to the core.

If you are to begin the process of removing the sin layers from your life, you will find the job far easier if you concentrate your efforts on becoming closer to the Creator and using His enormous strength in the effort, instead of concentrating on changing the behavior itself using only your own power.

Embrace Your "Work" with Enthusiasm, Integrity, and Pride

Who can not hear the selfish, anguished cry throughout the land complaining about the prevailing "Christian (or puritan) work ethic," just as they have about puritan ideas of sexual morality. The result of this sea change in thinking is a generation or two of workers who don't enjoy their jobs, could care less about the quality of the effort, and take advantage of their employers or their customers at every turn.

You need to teach your children, by your words and your example, that work is enriching, man's natural calling, and should be immensely rewarding. It will only be so, however, to the extent that the worker pursues his employment, family commitments, or charitable efforts with joy, enthusiasm, dedication, and integrity.

Not too long ago, my wife Pam and I laughed long and hard at a cartoon that appeared in our local paper. It showed scene after scene of kids expressing their unhappiness over having to perform some chore. "Do I hafta?" "You mean the whole room?" "But Mommmm!" Anyone who has kids, or who has even been near one, has heard these plaintive cries. Eventually, one of the cartoon parents wonders aloud to the other, "Why do these kids whine about everything we ask them to do?" This question was followed by three or four additional frames with the parents exclaiming: "All I ever do is wash dishes!" "I hate doing these bills!" and "It's your turn to change his diapers!" "No, it's not. I did it this morning."

Am I proposing that each one of us is going to suddenly love every aspect of our jobs, or house-cleaning, or child-rearing? Not if I hope that you will take anything else I say seriously. However, the end of the Christian work ethic brought about an end to the teachings of how we can make work fun. We used to be taught to make work a game. "Busy hands are happy hands," my grandmother said. She also repeated as often as necessary, "Idle hands are the devil's workshop." Today we stress the importance of leisure and recreation to escape from work. However, it is commonly through this leisure that we seek to indulge ourselves in those things my grandmother meant in her reference to the devil's workshop. This is not meant to suggest that we should be all work and no play, to invite another old saying to the party. The goal should be to find such satisfaction in our work that our diversions are just that, not escape. Moreover, the play side of our life should be mindful of the opportunity for inappropriate behavior to fill it.

Respect for one's employer seems to be another lost concept. While bosses have probably never been totally free from the negative view of those who have commanded the cultures of history, I think the picture painted of employers today is so overwhelmingly negative that it is creating divisiveness between the supervisors and the supervised. Look at the pervasiveness of workman's compensation fraud and the clamor for taxation of the rich. The media (themselves employers) show the owners getting rich off the sweat of the employees but forever fail to point out the risk, the hard work, or the tragedy of failure that the "rich" owners go through.

If we are to truly enjoy our work, we must appreciate those who have provided us with a place to work and a paycheck. In order to do that, we need to have a predisposition of respect for those who have created the companies and built them to their present stage. If those owners or managers should later prove to be unworthy of our respect, it should be a signal to object, in hopes of changing the situation. Failing that, we should be prepared to take our talents and resources elsewhere, not create additional problems for those who remain.

Be Trustworthy, Honorable, and Chivalrous

These notions seem hopelessly outdated today. We seem to have replaced them with "Do what you want," "Where is the loophole?" and "Me first." It is so unusual today to find people who are looking out for someone else's interest that they stand out in a crowd. We must teach our kids that this is backwards. It should be the person whose only care is for themselves who looks out of place.

We were taught to help old ladies across the street, stand up and give ladies our seat, and see to it that women and children were first off a sinking ship. Today, we not only fail the first two tests, we want to put our women on the front lines to die for us in battle. Surely it is a messed-up society that thinks this way.

Contracts and commitments should be carried out in the spirit in which they were intended. Today we pay lawyers thousands of dollars to help us break our promises. We pay still more to get out of paying our debts when we have spent beyond our means. It is only the rare individual who feels compelled to pay those debts no matter how long it takes or what kind of sacrifice is required.

Even while we are walking away from our own commitments, maintaining that we are not responsible for our actions, we turn around and sue anyone who seems to have transgressed us in even the smallest way. We take advantage of businesses, insurance companies, and government in our greedy attempt to gain at their expense. We look the other way as employees steal on the job. We laugh at the fraudulent claims made by our neighbor on his insurance claim. We read with less and less amazement about how many kids cheat on their exams, would keep found money, and engage in every conceivable illegal and illicit activity.

Your example in these areas is likely to lead your children and others to want to emulate you. Will it be negatively or positively? Are you teaching these values to your kids? Do you believe that the schools are? Without these fundamentals in place, we cannot hope to maintain a just society.

Obedience to Authority

Recognizing on the one hand that there are so many laws today about every aspect of our lives that it is hard to keep up with what we are supposed to do, we still must teach and practice obedience. Our answer to bad law today is to ignore it rather than try to change it. If we fail to teach obedience of even the smallest, least important laws, we invite every member of society to decide for themselves whether or not to obey the most important of our statutes. The result of a failure to teach obedience is anarchy.

Stopping short of developing an entire book on this subject, we do have an obligation to disobey when the law is contrary to God's law. This may be seen in some of the civil disobedience that took place to insure that our laws be applied equally to each of our citizens, regardless of color. It can be seen today in the efforts of pro-life groups protesting in front of abortion clinics.

The important element here is that children must be taught to obey their parents, teachers, police officers, and

others in authority. Then above all, they must obey God.
Even this obedience has its very practical side. To the extent
that everyone obeys the rules, the rest of us have a greater
ability to predict the behavior of those around us. This then
creates more peace of mind and peace in the community.

Love

The great commandments are: "Love the Lord your God
with all your heart and with all your soul and with all your
mind. . . . Love your neighbor as yourself" (Matt. 22:37-39,
NIV). If we as individuals, families, communities, and a nation were only able to obey the two great commandments,
we could do away with all that I have written until now. In
fact, we could do away with most laws. If each of us forgot
our own schedules, lusts, desires, and agendas just long
enough to walk in the shoes of our neighbor, we would have
an amazing world.

But, unfortunately, we don't teach or model love. We
teach and model greed, self-centeredness, "us vs. them," and
the quest for more and better stuff. No man or boy who
truly loved a young girl or woman would subject her to sex
before marriage. There is no possibility that he is doing that
for her; he is only thinking of himself.

There is no possibility that those who are putting their
love for others ahead of themselves would ever abort a child.
Besides the end to life of the innocent, there is also the
potential damage to the mother, father, parents, and even
the doctors and nurses involved in the abortion who may see
their error at a later time.

No woman who loved her neighbor as herself would ever
induce a young man to have sex with her in order to entrap
him into a relationship. Nor would she sleep with any man,
married or not, who wasn't her husband, knowing the harm
that would certainly come to spouses, children, and other
relations around both families.

No parents for whom the love of others is their highest
commitment would ever break up their family through divorce because they "don't love the other person." This failure to love the partner is their own, not that of the other
person. Their decision will bring great harm to their chil-

dren and to others around them and can only be the result of self-centered and unloving motives. (Certainly there are situations in which abuse, addictions, and other extreme problems might make even the unfortunate aspects of divorce superior to continuing in the abusive situation; however, most divorces today have nothing to do with such extreme behavior.)

What Can We Do?

I know there are hundreds of thousands of men out there who can pass the above test. Maybe you'd only deserve a *B* or a *C–*, but you also intend to bring your grade up. You have to be as mad as I am at what's happening today. If you want to help make a difference, you have to have a strong spiritual grounding. Those who are thus prepared need to come together to fight this battle. It won't be won by a disorganized effort, because the other side is powerful and very well organized. We need to provide a united front of individuals who share certain common ideas. Through this united front we can break the back of the enemy and scatter his remains in the battlefield.

If you want to be part of the army; if you are spoiling for a good fight; if you love your wife, mother, and kids, and are tired of their well-being and even their lives being constantly at risk; if you believe the time has come to take back our culture from the morally confused and the sexually deviant and return America and other Western cultures to a time when right was right and wrong was wrong; turn to chapter 10 and see the battle plan unfold.

TEN

The War to Restore Sexual Sanity

❖

"The people who went back to see 'Pretty Woman' four or five times were 13- and 14-year-old girls," says Joan Scott, president of the Writers and Artists talent agency. *"And the message they got was—what's so terrible about prostitution? It even looked glamorous."*

Patrick Goldstein,
L.A. Times Calendar Section
18 April 1993

My good friend, Elton, is pushing thirty. Mutual lady-friends tell me he is very, very cute. He is so charming and gracious that he has rarely been turned down for any job, even in a recession, regardless of his so-so employment history. He loves to work out with weights and is almost always in top physical condition, both in health and looks. He is smart, energetic, and enthusiastic. When I first met Elton, I believed he would have great success in his life.

Elton had a child out of wedlock about ten years ago. He worships the ground she walks on. He and the mother set up housekeeping for some time but never married. They ended this relationship several years ago. Elton has just recently told me that he is dating again, and that for the first time in a long time he took out a young woman, and they had sex. They had known each other for a week. She didn't request or require a condom. Elton insisted they use one. You see, Elton is HIV positive.

He was amazed that she didn't inquire about his sexual health status in this world of sexually transmitted disease. He said he felt she was a real "slut" to be willing to go to bed with someone without even asking that question and without requiring the use of protection.

HIV and the near certainty that he will contract AIDS has ruined his life. He doesn't work because he is afraid that the stress could shorten his life. He knows that the relationship with the mother of his child ended at least in part because of the "mistake" he made that resulted in HIV. He knows that his possible early death will mean his darling daughter won't have a daddy to raise her.

In the face of all this, Elton said to me, "It isn't reality for me not to have sex. It isn't reality for me and my friends to hope for a life where two people marry, have children, and live their lives together, forever. We just can't do it."

I asked him whether he has ever done drugs. "Oh, no! I would never do that."

"How is it then," I inquired, "that the discipline you have to avoid drugs fails you in the area of sex and marriage?" He had no answer.

The answer is clearly stated in his cry, "It isn't reality." In other words, he has not been taught that this can be achieved. His own family, his schools, and his ongoing education through TV, movies, records, and print media all tell him, "It isn't reality."

Today, I am calling on you to take a stand in the public arena. Today, I need at least ten million troops who will endure a bit of sacrifice: a few phone calls made or letters written; participation in a nationwide day of atonement; a spreading of the word to family, friends, neighbors, and co-workers; everyone in prayer—most of all, prayer!

But, with the exception of prayer, the key element in this effort is for ten million of us to vote with our remote controls and our pocketbooks. I want to provide you with a quotation from a *Los Angeles Times* opinion page article that confirmed my decision to mount this crusade. The title was, "Artists Must Declare Sides in the Nation's Culture War."

"What Dan and Marilyn Quayle fail to understand is that the American people have already taken sides in the culture war. The public casts its vote each time it turns on the TV, buys a record, reads a book or sees a movie or a play." You see, those who are destroying our civilization in the name of greed and personal irresponsibility believe that you and I are behind them all the way. And you know what? We often act like it. Today is the day I want you to take a pledge to join with ten million others to vote a new way.

First, I want you to agree with me that the media has gone too far. It is time to ask those who have such access to our lives and those of our children to be more responsible. The first effort will be directed at television. I am asking you, and as many like-minded as you can gather together, to turn off your television and discontinue your cable service. This will take place on 30 October 1993. We will continue this boycott until such time as the networks and cable providers agree to a new broadcast code. Support for this proposition comes from some unexpected places: *TV Guide* (21 November 1992, 16-17):

> Bill Clinton: I saw a show the other night on during the family hour, and I was just mortified. . . . I only saw four or five minutes of it. I was stunned.

Earlier in the same article,

> TV Guide: When you met with a large Hollywood group this summer you said, "Help us write the future." What did you mean?

> Clinton: That TV and movie makers could, without undermining their artistic integrity, have a major new impact on the way people view the world—giving people something to look up to, deglamorizing mindless sex and violence. . . . There's no question the cumulative impact of this banalization of sex and violence in the popular culture is a net negative for America. Historically, artists elevated humanity, they didn't debase life.

Hillary Rodham Clinton, "When It comes to Family Values . . . 'I Worry About Television,'" *Parade Magazine* (11 April 1993, 16):

> There has been a reinforcement by popular culture of

the undermining of social values. . . . I personally worry
more about television than other forms of entertainment, because it's a . . . value transmitter. . . . The low-
est-common-denominator quality of much of what appears on television and in other forms of popular
culture—the constant barrage of violence and explicit
sexuality—reinforces the loosening of human
bonds. . . . I don't think there's anything wrong with
parents' groups or other groups calling for people to
boycott certain kinds of entertainment. That's advo-
cacy, education, and choice.

The points of the proposed code are as follows:

1. In that television so dominates the way that our civilization learns about our world and everything in it, and in
that television has the ability to persuade great numbers of
people about the issues of the day, and in that television is
the single greatest source of the transmission of our culture,
it is critical to the future of a free and civilized nation that
those in the television industry be held to certain standards
of conduct.

2. In general, television should be providing only that
programming which will further the goals of our nation's
social contracts. Within the reality of acknowledged differences among people as to what might further such goals, we
believe that the following should represent the views of the
vast majority of Americans.

a) Violence is a part of our world, but peace is among
the highest goals among civilized people. Television should
never glorify or promote violence except in the principled
defense of our liberties. Those who act violently for other
reasons should always be seen as coming to justice for their
acts.

b) Illegal, immoral, and unethical behavior should never
be glamorized or promoted except in the context of civil
disobedience, and even then, within the bounds of civility
and decency. Criminal and antisocial action of all types should
be seen as having adverse consequences. This would include
the abusive use of drugs and alcohol.

c) Sexual intercourse outside the bounds of marriage
should never be promoted, glamorized, or endorsed. Those

who engage in such behavior should always be seen as making an irresponsible decision and should be the recipient of clear consequences.

d) The use of profanity of any kind should be ended.

e) The portrayal of women as sex objects, including nudity or near nudity, should be ended. Women should not be shown welcoming sexual violence, or to mean "yes" when they say "no."

f) Casual conversations between two or more opposite sex acquaintances that are full of sexual innuendo should be ended if the dialogue would tend to imply that women generally desire such attention from casual acquaintances.

g) No programming should promote or glamorize the homosexual lifestyle or acts. This is in no way intended to suggest that homosexual characters cannot be seen to be otherwise normal, happy people.

h) The showing of, or discussion of issues such as pedophilia, bestiality, incest, and other such behavior should never be shown or discussed within the context of entertainment programs. To the extent that they are used in news and information programming, they should always be seen to be abhorrent, antisocial behavior devoid of any benefit to the participants or society.

i) Television should be sensitive to all minorities and subgroups. However, this should in no way stop the use of innocent, humorous material that is not intended to in anyway malign or deride the target of the humor.

The timing of this boycott is critical. Each year the industry takes our pulse, or vote, on what old and new programming is working. They do this during the first weeks of the new season. The networks then use the results of this vote to sell their advertising. If our army can convince the advertisers that we aren't going to watch smutty, violent, and irresponsible programming any more, you can be certain that they will bring all the pressure necessary to change the content immediately.

If you are reading this after 30 October 1993, there is still plenty to do. Keep reading.

Some of you are already thinking about the sacrifice of not watching your television: No sports, CNN, soap operas, or cartoons for the kids. Unfortunately, this war can't be won without sacrifice. The networks, producers, and stars should be very concerned about the long-range consequences. The boycott might result in families who learn to read, talk, and play together, or lend their talents to community service instead of vegetating in front of the tube.

The more of you who pledge to participate in the boycott and actually follow through, the shorter the sacrifice will be. But even if it takes a month, three months, or longer for the enemy to see it is beaten, surely turning off the TV is a minor inconvenience compared to sending your son off to war or standing in front of approaching tanks. Those are the kinds of sacrifices people have had to make in the past to stop an enemy bent on destroying the cultural underpinning of their community or nation.

Most of the people that I talk to who are in agreement with these positions don't watch much television anymore, in any case. When their kids watch TV, they feel they must be in the room to monitor the content. Turn the box off with me on 30 October. Stand up and be counted. Care enough about your kids' and grandkids' futures to stop the teaching of immorality in our own living rooms.

Second, if you want to do even more, there are many groups throughout the United States who are already boycotting companies who have been most evident in their support for programs with illicit sexual content or excessive violence. You may wish to join in one or more of these boycotts as well. One of the most successful has been Dr. Don Wildmon's Clear TV. You can reach this organization by writing to: American Family Association, 214 Massachusetts Ave. NE, Suite 500, Washington DC, 20070.

Third, on 1 December 1993, I am asking you to take the next step. Our country needs your commitment to refuse your movie patronage to any theater that isn't willing to agree to a new code regarding the content of movies and previews shown in that theater. The pre-Christmas movie season has been selected because it is very critical to the movie industry. Please continue this boycott until such time as your local theater or theaters agree to the new code. It would differ from the TV code only in the following ways:

2(d) The use of profanity of any kind should be limited to contexts where the plot would be irretrievably damaged for failure to use it; and 2(j) The showing of explicit sexual interaction should be eliminated.

This boycott must be locally monitored, even though the effort will be made nationwide. The most effective work will be done working with the owners of independent theaters and small chains. If one theater in your neighborhood can be persuaded to agree to the code, the victory is in hand. If you had a theater where you knew you could go, and where you could send your kids with certain knowledge that the content would not be detrimental, you would be far ahead of the current state of affairs.

To the extent that those theaters are the most successful at the local level, and films which meet the code are consistently the most successful at the national level, the industry will eventually wake up to the economic reality. Some hope is already evident in a comment by Jack Valenti, president of the Motion Picture Association of America, as reported by the Associated Press on Wednesday, 10 March 1993: "We have to increase the theater audience—we just have to do it." He predicted that filmmakers would start making pictures with "less violence, less sensuality, and less language." He added, "You have to bring in a family audience." This is the same Jack Valenti who shortly after he became president of the MPAA junked the Hays Code which set the kind of guidelines in the past that might bring back the family audience today. Maybe Jack should say he's sorry, he messed up, and put the code back into practice.

Unfortunately, even as one of the top leaders of the industry shouts this message, those in the industry don't seem to hear. Michael Medved, a well-known movie critic and television personality, reports at length about the suicidal nature of Hollywood's pandering in filth in his book *Hollywood vs. America.* He shows how ticket sales have dropped off dramatically since the movies began emphasizing sex, nudity, and depravity of every stripe. He shows how time and time again the best attended movies each year are the G- and PG-rated movies, while on average, the PG-13 and R-rated offerings don't make as much money.

Through this boycott, we can have a true win-win situation. We can improve our society through teaching appropriate behavior, increase the availability of good entertainment, and increase the profits of the movie studios.

Fourth, the third boycott is one I would especially hope to call off before it happens. I believe that the Disney organization is one of the few bright lights in an otherwise bleak landscape of entertainment companies. Unfortunately, even they seem to have become caught up in this idea that you need to inject sex and sleaze into their product to sell it. This seems odd in that they were quite successful in the past with truly wholesome content, and their big winners of the late eighties and early nineties have been such films as *The Little Mermaid*, *Aladdin*, and the re-release of *101 Dalmations*. The Disney capitulation seems particularly troubling because parents have always trusted Disney to provide wholesome entertainment. If they are willing to violate that trust in small ways now in pursuit of "art" or a few extra bucks, then we as parents must reevaluate our trust in them.

If Disney is unwilling to adopt a code with regard to their various productions—in particular, Touchstone pictures, Hollywood pictures, and the Disney Channel—we will ask you to help by boycotting all Disney parks and products as of 15 June 1994.

Fifth, as a part of these efforts, I would ask you to send letters or make phone calls to various network officials, program producers, local station owners, cable company management, television stars, and advertisers in an effort to prove to them that they should agree to the new code because it is right, and failing that, they should sign on to the code in the interest of avoiding financial ruin.

Many of you could write many incredible letters from your own knowledge and the materials in this and other books. On the other hand, one acquaintance of mine said she "can't even write a letter to a friend." For those of you in that category, use the following ideas to help inspire your writings.

> I greatly enjoy much of what I see on television today. Unfortunately, almost every show has some material that I find offensive.

I am offended when:

1. Swear words and curses are used which I don't allow in my home. I don't want my children to use these words, but it is hard to teach them when TV is doing the opposite.

2. Preteens, teens, and young unmarrieds discuss sexual topics or participate in sexual activities where the end result is that it's acceptable for these groups to be sexually active. With all the negative consequences of promiscuity, I can't understand why TV would want to teach our kids to have sex before marriage.

3. Women are shown to be mere sex objects or toys who are just waiting for some hunk to get them into bed. It's no wonder that young men in school and older men in the work place think it's OK to harass women.

4. Violence of any kind is seen to be the best or only solution. If we believe that Western society is the pinnacle of civilization, shouldn't we be teaching that violence should only be the last resort and only in the most limited of circumstances?

5. Sex and violence are combined. How can the women of America ever feel safe if men are being shown that women "like to be raped," or that violent sex is exciting?

6. Blacks, Asians, Indians, foreigners, the clergy, religious people, gays, parents, political leaders, policemen, or any other groups are made fun of in a mean-spirited way. It is possible for people of taste to kid others about their behavior without doing it in a mean-spirited manner.

7. Women are shown nude or near nude for the express purpose of sexual titillation of my husband or son.

I will participate in the nationwide boycott of all television that will begin with the new season. I will discontinue my subscription to the local cable network. I will only return my patronage to the television industry when that industry shows that it is sensitive to my needs and concerns as outlined in the proposed code.

Sixth, finally, we want your kids to return all their records, tapes, and CDs that include lyrics that portray sexually inappropriate themes. This might include disrespect for sexual partners or glorification of illegal or immoral behavior such as rape, assault, or incest. On returning these materials indicate that if you are refused full credit you will bring a legal action against the store for having sold this material to a minor.

Ask your kids to send a letter to any local radio station which plays such music or whose radio "personalities" are so lacking in anything of significance to say that they must resort to smutty language and inappropriate subject matter. In this letter they should indicate their decision to boycott that station until it can meet a code of common decency.

These then are the efforts we intend to level at the entertainment industry. They will scream censorship, but it is no such thing. The media delivers a product. It is our right to decide what product we buy, whether lettuce, cable TV, or R-rated movies. It is illogical for any person to spend money or time on things which will harm them or their families.

The most important boycott will be the first one. First, because we will be taking on the great one-eyed monster who rules our homes. Many will question whether we will be effective at getting ten million people to give up this habit. Second, it will be the most important because it is the first one. If we are successful with television, the movie industry will likely go quietly. Disney will undoubtedly put up a white flag early. This will only leave the radio and record industries. They will definitely be the most difficult, but if boycotting doesn't work, we have a few other ideas up our sleeve.

The TV boycott is critical to the success of the entire effort; therefore, our future as a great nation, your children's future well-being, and your unborn grandchild's hope to ever see the light of day all depend on your willingness to make this sacrifice.

I call first on the men as the spiritual head of the household to bring your families together and explain the importance of this cause. You will undoubtedly find that if you are willing to replace the television with games, reading aloud, family discussions and devotions, and trips to local museums, parks, and playgrounds, your kids will probably hope the TV never goes back on.

Moms, if your husband isn't willing to lead this effort, please get his agreement to support your interest in making a better future for your kids. Tell him how scared you are to be on the street alone knowing that there are men out there who have just watched a porn movie showing a woman enjoying rape and torture.

Kids, if your folks are so wrapped up in their sports, sitcoms, and game shows that they can't see the harm that the current message is creating in our society, tell them what's really going on at your high school. Tell them which of your friends are sexually active, suffering from STDs, or have had abortions. Maybe you'll even have to tell them where you are sexually to wake them up to reality.

You may wonder whether we, united in this way, can be effective. Dr. Richard Neill, a dentist in Fort Worth, Texas, has been playing David to a major television Goliath, Phil Donahue. This one-man, political action committee started sending transcripts of the "Donahue Show" to various sponsors of the program. He complained that the material was not appropriate for children and that many children were home at the time the "Donahue Show" came on the TV.

To date, over two hundred sponsors have discontinued their support for the show. If one Dr. Neill can have this kind of an effect, imagine what a few million of us might accomplish.

You've read all this material, and you agree with the need and are willing to join. You still wonder how it will be possible to get ten million people to become part of the movement. Radical action requires radical approaches. The next chapter will explain how you can become a part of the largest network in the world.

ELEVEN

Defining the Enemy

———————— ❖ ————————

CBS Broadcast Group President Howard Stringer told an industry conference that violence has risen to such proportions that it has become "hard not to think we had some role" in the conditions leading to it. He said programs that contain gratuitously violent scenes probably contribute to the cynicism some young people have for others.

Skip Wollenberg,
Santa Monica Outlook,
24 March 1993

During the 1992 presidential campaign, a new phrase became a hot issue, the "cultural elite." For all the attention it received, the various politicians, reporters, and commentators seemed to have difficulty defining who this phrase was meant to define. A broad definition would include "those who, by reason of their status through position, power, or wealth, have the ability to impose their cultural agenda on the less powerful."

Conservatives first used the phrase, and they intended the meaning to be of a narrower focus. The proposition they asserted is as follows: Due to the lopsided representation of those with a liberal viewpoint in the press, the television industry, and the movie business, individuals who held a conservative view of culture were effectively being locked out.

The evidence of this phenomenon is overwhelming. The liberals would hardly deny it. And as a result of the liberals

177

gaining control of both the executive and legislative branches in 1992, those who are hoping to stop the nation's continuing slide into moral decay have even less voice.

Numerous leaders on both sides of the cultural divide have referred to this struggle as a war. I have used terms of war to describe the action that I believe we should take against the liberal, cultural elite. Thus, in continuing the analogy, those who believe in promoting sex outside of marriage, pornography, homosexuality, abortion on demand, incest, sexual violence, women as sex objects, bestiality, and pedophilia are defined as the enemy.

As we begin this war in earnest, we must keep in mind that there are those in every group or industry who are clearly our allies. Thus, while most major newspapers are clearly liberal, there are some like the *San Francisco Examiner* that wish to restore a value-centered America.

Even within the television industry, there are those who hold to our views. I would have much preferred to call for a limited boycott of television so that we could applaud those programs, cable stations, producers, and stars who stand for sexual responsibility and the humanization of women.

Unfortunately, after much consideration, it was clear to me that any boycott must send an uncomplicated message. The entire industry must clean up its act. Otherwise, we will still be in a position, as parents and grandparents, of having to continuously monitor the content of the programs our children watch.

TWELVE

How Can You Help?

---------------- ❖ ----------------

Your participation is vital. You can do just a little, or you can jump in with both feet and become a leader. The first step is the same as with any other trooper in any other war. America needs you to sign up and become part of the greatest network in the world.

By sending us the form included at the back of this book you will state your agreement with millions of other Americans that the media must show responsibility in the content of its programming. You are also agreeing to participate in the television boycott by turning off your televisions and ending your cable subscriptions on 30 October. You further agree to leave your TV off as long as it takes to get the networks, producers, and others who determine the content of television to agree to a new code.

You will notice that we ask you for your address, phone numbers, fax numbers, and other information. This information will be used only to further the purposes of this effort.

We will be using the most advanced technologies possible to create a massive information network. As Chuck Colson admonishes us in his recent book, *The Body*, "Finally, we must learn how to support and encourage one another. If we are to be the agents behind enemy lines, then it is critical that we establish a network whereby Christians can pass information back and forth to one another."

The goal will be to have three million active families on the network. With an average of over three persons per family, we will have our ten million workers and fighters.

Through this network, we will be able to communicate a request for action to all ten million of you in a single day.

Once an action has been agreed upon, the network will go into action. Our intention is to have at least fifty thousand folks nationwide who are accessible by fax machine. Fax messages will be sent out by computer in local areas so that most or all of the calls made by the computer will be free. If you are an area co-coordinator, you might send out one hundred such faxes from your computer after having received your instructions through another part of our network. A neighborhood coordinator would receive this fax message from the area coordinators. The neighborhood coordinator might then have a list of ten people to call with that day's action. One hundred fifty thousand who then reach ten each makes 1.5 million families.

As a worker, you might receive a telephone call asking you to write a letter to a specific station, producer, actor, or other entity within the entertainment field. Or you might also be asked to contact a congressman, senator, or even the White House. Possibly, on a certain day, the entire network would wear white arm bands to show how many there are of us.

If you have a computer, we'll ask you to get hooked up with a modem to Prodigy, the largest of the computer networks. Through this network you will be able to access a special bulletin board where you can receive news of the boycott and instructions for additional action. You then might be an area coordinator who faxes through your computer to one hundred local co-coordinators. Or you might be asked to call the major church leaders in your area.

Others of you will receive their updates through E-Mail. Each day you will call a local or 800 number to find out what's going on. Some days there will be a specific request to take action. Your action could be any of the ones described above for those who are in the computer network, fax network, or phone network. Our goal is to have 150,000 people like you checking their E-Mail each day and then contacting ten people with the next action.

To insure that we build the army to these proportions, we will also use radio. We are asking all talk show hosts to

pass the word along to their listeners as to what each new
action is. Will all talk show personalities agree? It would be
a great miracle if they did. However, we are praying that
many religious and conservative personalities and commentators who have the ear of thousands and even millions will
want to help in this endeavor.

If you and the other 9,999,999 like-minded souls quickly
respond to each of these instructions, the impact will be felt
across the land. Many individuals and companies who are
blatantly attempting to profit by exploiting sex and violence
have been faced with a few hundred letters from irate consumers before. Imagine the impact of ten million working
together. What would the president of a corporation think
if we can send him hundreds of thousands of letters from
those who buy his products?

Now imagine this. What kind of power could we bring
to bear on the peddlers of smut if we were able to have ten
million people praying for an end to sex and violence on TV
on a single day?

Please tear out the form at the back of the book, fill it
in, and mail it today. Don't delay even one day. Every minute
counts. We need your help now, not next week.

There are two copies of the form. Please tear both out
and have copies made. Ask friends, church members, and
co-workers to fill out the copies you've made and send them
in as well. You may also want to give them a second copy to
make copies, etc. *Please make copies of the form, fill one out, and
mail today!*

Another way that you can have a major impact on this
effort is to help persuade other organizations of which you
are a part to support the call for a boycott. This might
include your local church, synagogue, or other religious
groups. Or possibly you are a member of a community
service organization such as Optimists, Rotary, or Lions.
Other possibilities might include chamber of commerce,
junior chamber, sororities, fraternities, business groups,
prayer groups, PTA, children's clubs, and organizations such
as boys' and girls' clubs.

If you belong to any such group, propose to the leadership of that organization that they pass a resolution support-

ing the boycott and its intention to establish a new television content code. If such a resolution is passed, please send it to us so that we may send out press releases to that effect. Some organizations of this type may not be able to pass a resolution as an organization. In those cases, ask that all the members sign individually: "We, the members of the South St. Club, agree that . . ."

You may also have certain civic organizations that will join the effort. City councils, school boards, and pension funds have been on the front lines of battles to end apartheid in Africa and other similar causes. Surely they should find this issue to have a greater impact on their own communities. I can't imagine there being a government official (elected or not) who would not want to see less teen pregnancy, more respect for women, less violence and hooliganism in our streets, and a return to a system of universally held values. We've tried the libertine method for thirty years. It hasn't worked. Our representatives should be ready to try something radical—like responsibility.

If you are successful in advancing a resolution with any local government that agrees with the call for a new television code and/or the boycott as a method of reaching that goal, let me know as soon as possible so that we can get the news out to the media.

Through the months of September and October, concentrate all of your effort on the television boycott. Don't be distracted by the movie theater action. While the television effort is going forward, various individuals will be in contact with those in the movie industry in an attempt to avoid the need for that boycott. If that second boycott needs to go forward, you will be informed through the network.

We will be organizing all parachurch organizations such as Christian Film and Television Commission, Human Life International, Traditional Values Coalition, Campus Crusade for Christ, and others, plus the major denominations, in a coordinated effort to provide real exposure to the movement. This will further increase the potential to reach our ten million goal.

We desire to reach the top five hundred individual churches in the country to repeat steps two and three above and to visit them personally or develop a corps of individuals who can reach them. If you would like to be a part of this corps, please write to me personally.

Always make it clear that every action taken by those in the network should be an expression of love. We should not be seen as raving lunatics, but as concerned citizens. We should not be tearing down, but building up. We should not be a part of the problem, but through our witness, lead others in the community to see the right way to live.

For this to work, the nation must see that the Lord's army is larger than the U.S., NATO, and Russian armies together: ten million strong.

It might be tough, but we want to contact as many non-Christian sects (Arabs, Muslims, etc.) and ask them to join in the action, as well as make contact with non-religious organizations for their support. Our goal is to make this a movement that goes beyond the so-called religious right. Just because the major leaders of this action are Christian, there is no intention to be exclusionary. We would expect that anyone who has an understanding of basic morality will see the wisdom in what we are fighting for.

Begin letter-writing campaigns, both to the editor of your local and regional newspapers as well as to magazines you subscribe to.

If you like to speak in public, develop a talk around the information in this book and try to arrange opportunities to speak in front of community organizations, parent-teacher groups, and civic clubs.

If you are politically inclined, you may want to try to bring pressure on city, county, state, or even the federal government to increase the regulation of various media through legislation. However, I generally feel we will have a better result through the marketplace.

If you have legal skills you might wish to sue businesses in your area which you believe are violating local laws against prostitution, pandering, pornography, or selling various kinds of illegal materials to minors.

Some groups have been very successful in persuading local newspapers to refuse advertising for offensive films.

Maybe we could request that they refuse to advertise offensive TV, radio, and records.

Local businesses are even more sensitive to boycott. If one or more companies in your local area are advertising their products on offensive shows, making or selling offensive materials, or helping the exploitation of women or children, ask them to discontinue their effort. If they refuse, get a group of people from the network to help you boycott or picket them.

THIRTEEN

Training the Troops

❖

If you are among the body of concerned citizens, I urge you not to just sit there. Get out and work for what you believe. . . . Write the producers and sponsors of sex and violence on television. . . . Pray for your country every day. . . . And by all means, do these things in a spirit of love that would be honoring to the One who sent us.

> Dr. James Dobson and
> Gary L. Bauer,
> *Children at Risk*

In order to maximize the potential for success in this campaign, those who endorse the intentions outlined in this book should try to speak with one voice. Moreover, that voice should be calm, not shrill; reasoned, not hysterical; and informed, not ignorant. The following materials will provide a synopsis of the arguments, some suggested letters, and a list of dos and don'ts for written as well as public presentations.

The press, especially television, will attempt to paint those of us who believe in sexual morality as right-wing extremists, or worse. It is unlikely that it will be possible to find many unbiased forums. If any of our members are asked to participate on a talk or news program, it is very likely that the host or editors will do their best to make us look foolish or to "cut" our strongest arguments and appeals from the tape.

Therefore, it is so very important that you have your facts well learned, your opinions well formed, and your ar-

guments well thought through before you venture into a
public debate. The facts in this book plus those presented in
other books on this subject will likely be all you need. I have
taken great pains to only recommend those works whose
research is impeccable and documentation is thorough. Read,
read, and read some more to prepare for any letters you
send or speaking you plan to do.

I would never presume to impose my opinions on you.
However, allow me to attempt to provide some succinct
statements that you may wish to use as a basis for some of
your opinions. Remember, if we have ten million totally
different ideas out there, it will be difficult for the rest of the
citizenry to focus on our message.

Basic Principle #1

Our leaders and those who have the greatest impact on
reaching culture through the media have decided in recent
years to move from a position of promoting cigarettes and
drugs to a position of discouraging their use. In the same
time frame, those same institutions have moved from a position of discouraging sex outside of marriage to promoting
and encouraging premarital sex, adultery, promiscuity, and
homosexual sexual activity.

We believe that if the national leadership and the media
were to use the same approach with sexual subjects as they
have with tobacco and drug use, it would have the same
impact on usage among teens and young adults as it did with
tobacco and drugs.

Basic Principle #2

Women are not sexual objects, playthings, or doormats.
They are much more likely than men to suffer severe damage to their physical, emotional, and spiritual health as the
result of illicit sexual behavior. Much of the current content
of television, movies, records, and radio encourage men to
have little respect for women. This lack of respect and inappropriate stereotyping of women's sexual wants or needs
also leads to inappropriate male behavior such as harassment, date rape, rape, assault, torture, and murder.

A secondary result of the increase in aggressive male
behavior toward females is that women live in constant fear

of such attacks in their communities and even in their homes. Our cultural leaders decry the results while stimulating the perpetrators. It is time that they acknowledge the cause-and-effect relationship. Stop portraying women as ready to go to bed with any "friend" within a few hours of meeting him. Stop showing women saying "no" and meaning "yes." Stop showing extramarital sex without consequence.

Basic Principle #3

The current societal acceptance of casual sex has resulted in a dramatic lowering of self-esteem in women who engage in this type of behavior. It is time to recognize that if our teens can give up drugs, cigarettes, or alcohol, they can give up sex.

Basic Principle #4

Every evidence suggests that the single mother family is a major part of the reason for increasing poverty, lawlessness, and feelings of loneliness in our society. The media has made what amounts to a constant assault on the institution of the family. Murphy Brown was only the final straw for many who saw early on what the President's Commission on the Family has only now reported. The "cultural elite" have helped to wreck the family. It is time that they begin to respect the most successful cultural grouping in every civilization. Alternative families are not equal to one mother, one father, and their natural children.

To call it better does not demean those who do not and can never have this preferable arrangement. By saying it is better, no one implies that it is perfect or that there are no single moms who are doing a better job at raising their kids than some "traditional" family units.

Our hats should be off to those who have been forced by circumstance to face the additional burden of having a broken family, but it is time for our leaders to become activists in helping rebuild broken homes and discouraging further break-ups.

Basic Principle #5

Society must operate on the basis of social contracts. We as citizens must contract with our government that we will follow the rules, pay our taxes, and accept its leadership. In our democracy we have the right to protest, leave, or vote the bums out. We don't have the right to just disregard. If we do, then we can't complain if our neighbor does. At that point, there is no contract left, only anarchy.

We must also have social contracts with regard to the way we treat one another. If I can treat you any way I please and vice versa, then I can't be sure that you won't shoot me for a nickel, and you can't be certain of me, either. If it is OK for me to sleep with your wife, then how can I trust you not to take liberties with mine?

The media has been preaching the gospel of do what feels good for an entire generation, and many decided that they liked that concept. Many of those who liked that concept are now dead, diseased, broke, or emotionally crippled because of folks who care more about themselves than others.

The leaders who repeatedly told us during the 1992 political campaign that character doesn't matter in a president were the ones who had it wrong. *They* didn't get it. Nothing else matters as much. We now have a president who cannot be trusted from one day to the next and a media who is congratulating him on his beautiful new clothes. They don't get it either.

Hopefully, the producers and presenters of sitcoms and drama can find the same heart for truth, charity, consideration, bravery, selflessness, and reverence for life that they have for whales and owls.

Basic Principle #6

Anyone who is willing to abort a child who would be viable outside of the womb unless the mother's life is in mortal danger can only be characterized as a heartless monster. It sickens me to imagine that any woman who has already felt her baby move in her womb would allow some man to earn money by ripping the child from her body.

It is appalling that we are killing 1.5 million unborn, defenseless babies per year because they would be an inconvenience to the mother or because in many, many cases the mothers are persuaded to such action by their boyfriend, husband, school counselor, or parents. I won't ask that all of us agree as to the government's role in ending this holocaust. The basic principle here would be that we all seek to reduce the number of abortions and increase the number of adoptions or other alternatives.

Currently, the media treat abortion as an operation with the same consequence as a wisdom tooth extraction. The average young woman is asked to believe that the fetus is just a blob of tissue. Might not the media call a baby a baby, whether born or not, and make the abortion decision one which should be taken only after careful deliberation and thorough consideration of the consequences now and in the future?

Our society takes the position that when we make a life-and-death decision about a multiple murderer, if there is any question, always decide in favor of life. Surely that should be our minimum attitude about an innocent unborn baby?

Basic Principle #7

If we are to have any hope of teaching our children that we should respect one another, shouldn't the entertainment industry make an effort to encourage respectful behavior and show the likely negative consequences of disrespectful behavior? Cussing, swearing, and profanity all depict total contempt. They are only used when people intend to be rude toward one another, or where vulgarity is socially "correct" (e.g., locker rooms and military camps).

The use of this language on the silver screen, the one-eyed monster, and over the radio waves is an insult to the listener, and teaches the impressionable that this is acceptable. As a student of language, I was always taught that the use of slang was a sign that the writer wasn't clever enough to find a better way to express the feelings of the moment. This would certainly indict most writers of popular material today.

Basic Principle #8

According to those who would deny America its rightful place in the sun, we are the most violent nation on the planet. Many of those who would agree with this idea are the same folks who know no bounds in showing graphic vio-lence, or who encourage violence through their songs.

Violence should be depicted as a final option, a last resort only to be applied when the harm or potential harm is great and the other methods of avoiding the harm have failed or have a low likelihood of success. Our children are being taught that violence is cool. Being tough and mean is the best. Heroes are not in style. The cultural elite who teach from this school ask, why is greed rampant? Why do our kids kill each other? Can you believe all the graffiti? Where are the heroes?

Basic Principle #9

Virtually no one wants their son or daughter to be a homosexual. In fact, it is likely that most parents would do almost anything to dissuade their children from such a path. Therefore, it would seem only natural that those who are delivering a product to consumers with that viewpoint would be sensitive enough to the consumer's feelings, hopes, and dreams that they would not purposely help to thwart these. It isn't necessary to condemn those who have homosexual inclinations in order to stop glamorizing their status. It is not an act of homophobia to show the truth about the negative consequences of being "gay." It doesn't demean anyone who is actively homosexual to promote abstinence. It may save their life! It isn't gay-bashing to promote mes-sages that most homosexuals can be cured. It isn't insensitive to be honest about the very normal reaction of a parent who learns that his child has a same-sex partner.

Basic Principle #10

Eighty-five percent of the U.S. population is Christian, or so they profess in the polls. Christians are a common target of the cultural elite. Negative stereotyping and bigotry that would never be tolerated against any other group is com-monly leveled against characters who take their Christianity seriously. America was a better place when more people took their Christianity seriously, and it would be a better place again if more did now. The church has a hard enough time trying to change the hearts of those who lack con-science or are filled with hate and self-destructive thoughts without TV and the movies discouraging people from getting closer to God.

Amazingly, many of my Christian friends encouraged me to talk less about the Christian aspect of this effort, for fear that readers would be offended by discussions of God and His ways. I make no apology for my beliefs to the 15 percent who don't believe the Bible. I hope this book will persuade you to turn to God, or at least to the wisdom contained in His Word.

Basic Principle #11

We've tried it your way, and it doesn't work. The experiment was interesting if destructive, bold yet lacking dignity, alluring but doomed to failure, as history has witnessed repeatedly. Sexual liberation, moral relativity, and irresponsibility didn't result in a better way of life. They have resulted in tragedy, death, and destruction.

We demand that those who wish to make money selling us their TV programs, movies, records, and radio shows end the social experiment *now*! The sexual revolution must end *now*. In its place must come responsibility and abstinence outside of marriage. Values must be reintroduced as part of a social contract that benefits everyone in society. We may not be able to agree on every single value, but there are plenty we can agree upon. Let's start there. Our young people and children must be taught the value of personal responsibility and accountability *now*. If the first target of our actions, the TV networks and cable providers, can't agree on this limited agenda, then we won't use their product. We will also try to avoid the products which are paying for the filth, the advertisers. Following are some examples of letters that you could write to several categories of individuals below. You would want to write these in your own words, add to or subtract from these ideas, or take a completely different approach. However, every letter should contain certain characteristics:

1. They should show concern or distaste for the action, but love and charity for the person who is acting in a way you deplore. For example: "I'm sure that you yourself are a good person, a loving husband, and a caring father. How-

ever, I wonder if you realize the impact that your action might have on my children."

2. Those who will be reading your letter may have an agenda and believe they are doing the right thing. If possible, try to include a personal experience to bring home your message. For instance: "My daughter is fourteen years old. Last Saturday night she went on her first date. Her boyfriend got mad when she said she wouldn't have sex with him, so he raped her." You may not have a story as poignant as that one, but any personal experience that lends credibility will work. Another example: "Last night I was watching TV with my fifteen-year-old daughter. We were so embarrassed by the constant talk about sex that we agreed to turn it off."

3. Bring in your authorities to support your arguments. Refer to this book or others, magazine and newspaper articles, or the statements of philosophical giants of history such as Christ, Moses, Plato, Socrates, St. Augustine, Bacon, Descartes, or Locke.

4. Always finish your letter with a clear statement of your request and the action you hope the reader will take. Here is the type of letter you might want to write to a producer of television programming.

Dear Mr. Producer:

    I am a single mother with three daughters, aged seventeen, fourteen, and twelve. It is one of my goals that each of them will enjoy their wedding night as a moment when they first experience sexual union. It is my belief that any act of premarital sex they might partake of will make this experience and their marriage less than it could have been.

    I also hope and pray that each of them will have the opportunity to maximize her opportunities in life. Each of them seems to have the abilities and desire necessary to get a college education and pursue good careers. How clear it seems to me that even a single error in the sexual area could destroy those dreams through sexual disease or pregnancy.

    As I watched one of the programs that you produced the other night, I had to wonder whether you have any daughters. I also wondered whether you had any similar hopes and dreams for them. I wondered whether or not you worried as I do that their chances hang by such a narrow thread. I don't know you or very much about you, but I imagine that you are a man of principle and good character. I suspect that you are concerned about the future of our nation and hope you care about those who watch your programming. As I watched this particular episode of your program, however, I was forced to tell the girls we would have to change the channel or turn it off. You see, the story line encouraged kids to have sex. Your characters weren't even eighteen and they decided it was OK to have sex. If your own daughter was watching, I suspect she would have been influenced in the direction of "go ahead and do it."

Would you be unhappy to learn that even one young lady who has her whole life ahead of her contracted a sexual disease because your show was the final argument she needed to go ahead and have sex? Would it concern you if hundreds of teen-age boys used this storyline to convince their fourteen- or fifteen-year-old girlfriends that they should give in if they really love him?

My request of you today is a simple one. Please make a minor change in the message you are sending. If an unmarried character is considering giving up his or her virginity, point out all the real potential consequences, the serious value issues, and don't ridicule the moral questions. Then have your star decide sex isn't worth the certain moral, emotional, and spiritual damage, or the potential physical, economic, and social disaster. Do it for me and my three girls or do it for your own daughters, nieces, or grandkids, but do it.

This could be a basic concept for one you send to a cable or network executive (use examples out of your own life):

Dear TV Executive:

My son, Jimmy, brought me some bad news the other day. It seems that his girlfriend is pregnant. He is the father. They are both fifteen, never get into trouble, and are excellent students.

They are now trying to decide what to do. None
of the answers are good ones. Jimmy believes deeply
that the embryo is a living human child and is quite
adamant that she have the baby, even if it means
giving it up for adoption. His girlfriend tends to agree
but has already cried about the idea of giving away
her baby.

Unfortunately for all, her dad is a prominent local
attorney. He is insisting on abortion. We're not certain whether he is more interested in her future or his
own. My son wants to know what this has to do with
a woman's choice.

I finally took them both aside and asked them
what had gotten into their minds. Why had they become sexually active? They explained that while both
sets of parents had made it clear that premarital sex
was both a sin and that there were many predictable
negative consequences, it just wasn't realistic for them
not to have sex. Their school, their friends, movies,
TV, records, and radio stations all had a different
story to tell than their parents: "Premarital sex is
something teens are going to do, and it's possible to
do it safely."

Their school showed them specifically how to have
safe sex. They tried it and liked it. They even used
condoms almost every time. But then one night . . .
you get the point. That one little mistake is sure
costing them now. I'm really angry, but not at them.
I'm angry that the message they received from the
programming on your station influenced them to take
this risk.

I'm asking you to think about this. Wouldn't it be
better to bring a message to our children that they
are very capable of exercising self-discipline when it
comes to their sexual desires? Would this be so different from the message we now send with regard to
cigarettes, drugs, or drinking and driving?

To be sure, there will always be those who don't
do what is best for themselves, for society, or what is
morally correct. Does that mean that we should abandon the principle for the rest of those who might

have the courage to do what is right if we adults just believe they could do so?

Please eliminate programming that encourages kids to have sex before marriage. Please include programming that shows the real consequences to such action.

This might be sent to a female director, producer, writer, or actress:

Dear Ms. Writer:

Every month about this time I think about you. I think about you as I endure the itching, searing pain that accompanies my herpes. I think about you because your powerful writing convinced me that I should join the sexual revolution. I don't blame you. I blame myself. However, I can't help but wonder how my life might have been different if I'd never seen one of your movies.

It wasn't clear to me if you were aware of the incredible toll sexually transmitted diseases (STDs) are taking on American women. I guess you'd be up to date on AIDS, but did you know that there are over twenty-five STDs at epidemic levels? Were you aware that three million teen-agers each year are infected with such diseases as herpes, pelvic inflammatory disease, new penicillin-resistant strains of gonorrhea, syphilis, chlamydia, and human papilloma virus (HPV)? That's just the teen-agers. This is according to the U.S. Department of Health and Human Services.

Will it surprise you to know that women are much more likely to be infected with an STD and that the effects of these diseases are substantially more severe for women than men? Do you know that women are experiencing everything from itching to sterility and cancer as a result of STDs; newborn children are being born with consequences of these diseases; and both children and adults of both sexes are dying from STDs?

I'm sure you believe that what you are doing is right. I have to imagine that you would not write materials that you suspected would harm people. I'm hoping that you are the kind of person who would rather believe that their work had resulted in one person being helped, than live with the possibility that even one had been harmed.

I am unable to imagine one benefit to the women of America that sex outside of marriage has created. I think of twenty-five diseases, thirty million abortions, countless children given up in adoption, and millions upon millions of relationship problems that have resulted from premarital and extramarital sex.

I'm calling on you to help our kids end their promiscuity and our adults to stay home with their spouses. Please say you'll help.

This letter might be sent to the publisher of sexually explicit (porn) materials.

Dear Publisher:

I wanted to write and tell you about the endless hours of pleasure that your products have provided me. Ever since I was a child I have spent hours reading sexually explicit materials, looking at pictures of naked women, and attending movies and stage shows where nudity and sexual acts were prevalent.

I wanted to let you know that I now find it much more gratifying to satisfy myself than to make love with my wife. She is not as beautiful as your women, and certainly not as young and supple. She isn't willing to do all the things the girls in your movies do either. There is no chance she'll let me have another woman join us in the bedroom.

Your products are so much more available than my wife is, too. Sometimes she says no, or isn't really into our lovemaking. I sometimes wonder whether she is aware that I have to fantasize about pictures I've seen in your magazines in order to enjoy sex. I know she doesn't like my interest in sexual materials. She says it hurts her that I look at these other women. She feels she should be enough for me.

I also want to mention that I used to think that when women said no, they meant no. You've been able to show me that women want really aggressive men in their lives. When they say no to my talk at the

office, I just push on, since I now understand it is just
a tease.

I know I'm not alone in many of these responses
to your material. The President's Commission on Pornography drew many of the same conclusions, and a
recent TV news program interviewed a group of men
who were having trouble with their sexual relationships as a result of their involvement with sexually
explicit material.

Finally, I want to let you know that my fourteen-
year-old son seems to be following in my footsteps.
He is spending almost all of his lawn-mowing money
on your stuff. I told him he shouldn't read it because
it might mess up his future sexual relationships with
women. He wasn't real ready to accept this idea from
a man who has boxes filled with the stuff.

I hope he doesn't find himself in the position of
needing more and more titillation. I know that I spend
a lot of my time now looking for a new twist that will
excite me. I'm kind of running out of ideas that can
be shown in two dimensions.

Thanks again for all your help.

Here is one that might go to a business owner or CEO
who advertises on TV:

Dear Mr. CEO:

I wanted to write to you and tell you how much
I like your products. I can see that you really care
about your customers. It shows in the quality and the
value of everything you sell. I suspect that you must
have some very strong personal values that have carried you to the position of leadership of a company
which offers such consistent quality.

Because I enjoy your products so much, I wanted
to let you know of my confusion with regard to another aspect of your company's thinking. How can
you support the sexual sleaze, excessive violence, disrespect for women, and promotion of a valueless society that is ever present in television programming
today? Your advertising continually shows up on some
of the most objectionable programming currently
being offered.

Because of my belief that you yourself have a strong value system, I would imagine that you are having to monitor your children's programming choices like I am. I don't know enough about you to know if you have kids at home. If not, you might want to call some of your friends or employees and ask them if they are concerned about what is being shown on TV. I suspect that you believe that women should be respected, but some of the shows you support concentrate most of their camera time on the breasts and legs of the actresses. Their characters commonly talk with casual male acquaintances in ways that suggest they want to go to bed with them. Some of your money is going to programs which suggest to my fifteen-year-old son that homosexuality is a great alternative to straight sex.

Are these the values that got you where you are today?

I am a part of the group that will be turning off their TV during the first week of the 1993 season. I'm encouraging all my friends to do so as well. I have not decided whether to stop buying your company's products yet, but unless you change your advertising policies, I will have no choice. You see, I can't allow my money to be spent by you in a way that could end up harming my own children. That would be plain stupid, wouldn't it?

Here is one that might be written to anyone in show business (use your own true-to-life example):

Dear Hollywood:

My name is Billy. I'm fifteen years old. My family just learned that my older brother has AIDS. This was a big surprise because we never thought he did drugs or was a homosexual. He's had lots of girlfriends.

It turns out he isn't gay. He does like girls. But after watching one of your programs at a friend's house, the friend convinced him to try some things with him just once. It turns out the friend was gay and had AIDS.

I read where lots of boys will have one or two homosexual experiences when they are teen-agers. I know I won't. I guess teen-age boys are likely to try almost anything once. Anyway, it seems like TV and movies today are glamorizing being a homosexual. I think it would be better if we were shown how to treat them nicely, but not encourage anyone to become that way.

I'm sure you didn't want my brother to get AIDS. But before somebody else experiments with this deadly activity, could you stop promoting homosexuality as a way of life? I also read where 75 percent of the psychiatrists say they believe homosexuals can be cured. Maybe you could do a show about gay men and women who are now straight. Maybe someone will write you a letter and thank you for turning their brother around before he got AIDS.

This might go to a congressman or senator (almost anyone can think of a personal example):

Dear Senator:

My sister's baby kept us up again last night. The baby is cutting teeth or something. I could probably have slept through the baby's crying, but my sister was yelling at the baby, and my mom was yelling at my sister.

My sister is sixteen. After she had the baby she moved out for a while, but she couldn't make it on her own, so she came back. She doesn't know who the baby's father is and doesn't care. She didn't want a husband; she wanted a baby. She says she wanted someone who would love her.

I'm fourteen, and one of the girls at school wanted me to give her a baby. I said no, but it was tempting. I saw an article in the *Los Angeles Times* view section on 13 March 1993 that talked about how lots of Latinos are doing this now. Other races, too, but lots of Latinos. The article said that we kids see 14,000 references to sex each year on TV, and only 140 even promote safe sex. I guess none talk about abstinence or what will happen to your life if you get pregnant or a disease.

My mom thinks part of the problem is that we don't have a dad. My sister's dad stopped seeing my

mom when he found out she was pregnant. My dad
used a lot of drugs and beat us up, so mom threw him
out. What I can't figure out is how come my sister
doesn't see that her kid isn't going to have a dad
either? Mr. Senator, it seems to me the government
isn't doing anything to keep families together. It looks
to me like TV and movies and stuff act like families
with only moms are just as good as ones with both a
mom and a dad. But I saw a small article about the
President's Commission on the Family, and it said the
main reason for poverty, drug addiction, gangs, and
violence in the inner city was broken families.

Can you and the rest of the senators come up
with some ideas of how to get families going again?
I've heard one or two that seemed pretty good. One
thing was to make divorce harder again. Another was
to make taxes favor families. Another was to make it
easier for moms to stay at home while their kids were
growing up. One more was to make sure dads who
leave their families help pay for the kids.

One more thing: Do you know anybody in Hollywood? Maybe you could ask them to only have ten
thousand sex scenes per year. Maybe five thousand
could be in favor of children having sex, and five
thousand against.

Here is a possible letter an adult could write to a congressman:

Dear Ms. Congresswoman:

My fifteen-year-old daughter just went out on a
date. I know every mom throughout history worried
when they sent their daughters out with boys they
knew almost nothing about. Somehow, I think things
are very different today, and I just had to write out
my feelings to you. When I was dating and my mom
was worried, she thought about a car accident; I think
about date rape. My mom peeked out to see if I
would get kissed on the doorstep. I picture my daughter undressed in the back of his car. My mom didn't
care much for our music. Today, my daughter may be
listening to music with that boy which tells him it's
OK to abuse her.

My mother had some concern that if I fell from grace I might get crabs, but they could be treated. I'm petrified that my little girl could end up with any one of twenty-five sexually transmitted diseases that could cause her pain and discomfort for life, render her sterile, result in her newborns being infected, or kill her.

If I'd gotten pregnant, my mom and dad would have been mad—real mad. But they would have eventually calmed down, and we would have discussed our options—keep the baby or give it up for adoption. If my child gets pregnant, she might be told by a school nurse to have an abortion—kill the baby—and never tell her dad or me. She might end up with an emotional scar from the killing of that fetus and from the secret. She might end up with physical scarring from the operation. She would never forget this decision she made without the loving counsel of her own mom and dad.

These two kids are pretty nice kids. They get good grades and don't get in trouble. Tonight they're going to see a movie. My mom didn't worry at all when I went to the movies except that he might put his arm around me. I worry that the movie I agreed to let them see will be sold out. They will make a reasonable decision to see another movie in the same complex. It will be one they are sure I would approve of. Unfortunately, I have frequently been surprised at the content of some PG-13 movies, and you never know what to expect from an R. I worry that this movie will get them all hot and bothered, and two otherwise good kids will get carried away.

There's more, but I've taken enough of your time. Surely there is something that our government can do to change attitudes about human sexuality. You people in Washington have been able to change attitudes about drugs, cigarettes, spotted owls, whales, homosexuals, and various kinds of prejudice. I bet if you put your mind to it, you could find some way to promote abstinence—maybe if we changed our spending priorities in Washington and spent $450 million on abstinence-based programs and only $8 million on contraception and safe sex instead of the other way around. I'm hopeful you share my concern.

I hope these letters will provide you with a basic approach to letter-writing that might be effective. They don't have to be this long. Sometimes a post card with fifty words will be more effective than a two-page letter. However, if we are to change the hearts of the people we are writing to, it will be necessary to make the letters up close and personal.

When you contact your E-Mail, look up the day's action on your computer, or receive a fax or phone call explaining the next activity of our ten million-member effort, there will always be a recommendation as to the approach to use and suggestions as to specific individuals and corporations to write to. You may want to send off a few letters of your own before or in between our other, more concentrated efforts.

A last thought: You can greatly increase your effectiveness through the use of computers. Even the least expensive word processor will allow you to write a single letter and then personalize it by changing just the header. You can make it appear even more personal by mentioning your correspondent by name in the body. The computer can be set up to automatically change that as well.

Maybe you thought only big companies could send out mass mailings with the personal touch, but you can do it, too. You could create a single "great" letter and with very little effort send it to dozens or even hundreds of people, and each one would have no way of determining if it was personal or not. To maximize your effectiveness during this campaign, may I recommend that you equip yourself with a word processor or computer that has this capability.

Our kids need *you*. Please pull the plug on your TV, cancel your cable subscription, and join this effort to win the cultural war. Don't believe that you can wait until next year. This is our big chance to unite and drive out those who would steal our culture.

Bibliography

❖

Benson, Peter, Dorothy Williams, and Arther Johnson. *The Quicksilver Years*. Cambridge: Harper and Row, 1987.

Covey, Steven. *Principle Centered Leadership*. New York: Summit Books, 1991.

Dobson, Dr. James. *Straight Talk to Men and Their Wives*. Waco, TX: Word Books, 1978.

Dobson, Dr. James, and Gary L. Bauer. *Children at Risk*. Dallas: Word, 1990.

Durfield, Richard C., and Renee Durfield. *Raising Them Chaste*. Minneapolis: Bethany House, 1991.

Guinness, Os. *The American Hour*. New York: Free Press, 1993.

Hattemer, Barbara, and Robert Showers. *Don't Touch That Dial*. Lafayette, LA: Huntington House, 1993.

Hughes, R. Kent. *Disciplines of a Godly Man*. Wheaton, IL: Crossway Books,1991.

McDowell, Josh. *What I Wish My Parents Knew About My Sexuality*. San Bernadino, CA: Here's Live Publishers, 1987.

McIlhaney, Joe S., Jr., M.D. *Sexuality and Sexually Transmitted Diseases*. Grand Rapids, MI: Baker Book House, 1990.

Marshall, Robert, and Charles Donovan. *Blessed are the Barren*. San Francisco: Ignatius, 1991.

Medved, Michael. *Hollywood vs. America*. New York: Zondervan, 1992.

Reisman, Dr. Judith A. *Soft Porn Plays Hardball*. Lafayette, LA: Huntington House, 1991.

Reisman, Dr. Judith A., and Edward W. Eichel. *Kinsey, Sex, and Fraud*. Lafayette, LA: Huntington House, 1990.

Strommen, Merton P. *Five Cries of Youth*. San Francisco: Harper Collins, 1988.

Strommen, Merton P., and A. Irene Stromen. *Five Cries of Parents*. San Francisco: Harper and Row, 1985.

Wright, H. Norman. *Understanding the Man in Your Life*. Waco, TX: Word, 1987.

I agree that the time has come for people of character to require an end to antisocial, antifamily, and immoral content broadcast over public airways and through public rights-of-way into my living room. I commit my family to turning off our television and discontinuing our cable service as of October 30, 1993, unless and until the networks, cable companies, and all others concerned agree to a new code of content.

I am also ready to offer my services as a soldier in this cultural war. Here is the information you will need to reach me with the developing strategy for a complete victory.

Signed: _____

Name: _____
Address: _____
Daytime phone number: _____
Evening phone number: _____
Fax number: _____

___ Can you use it for outgoing faxes?
___ Do you own a computer?
___ Will you equip it for Prodigy?
___ Number in your family.
___ How many are willing to be active?
___ Are you willing to call an E-Mail center each day to receive instruction?
___ I would like to be an area coordinator
___ I would like to be a local coordinator
___ I can do far more than that. I could devote full/half time to this work.
___ I am a pastor, deacon, or other leader of a church. I believe that I can persuade our entire church to become involved in this action.
___ I am a leader in a non-church organization (Rotary, YMCA, Optimists, Boys' Club, etc.). I believe I can persuade our organization to back this action.
___ I have made copies of this form and will encourage my friends, fellow church members, and co-workers to send it to you, also.
Other comments, ideas, or questions:
_____
_____
_____

Please fill in the form on the reverse side and mail to:

Coalition for the Code
P.O. Box 3086
Santa Fe Springs, CA 90670

Please remember to make copies and mail or give to friends, family, and associates at work, in your neighborhood, at church or to other groups.

I agree that the time has come for people of character to require an end to antisocial, antifamily, and immoral content broadcast over public airways and through public rights-of-way into my living room. I commit my family to turning off our television and discontinuing our cable service as of October 30, 1993, unless and until the networks, cable companies, and all others concerned agree to a new code of content.

I am also ready to offer my services as a soldier in this cultural war. Here is the information you will need to reach me with the developing strategy for a complete victory.

Signed: _____

Name: _____
Address: _____
Daytime phone number: _____
Evening phone number: _____
Fax number: _____

___ Can you use it for outgoing faxes?
___ Do you own a computer?
___ Will you equip it for Prodigy?
___ Number in your family.
___ How many are willing to be active?
___ Are you willing to call an E-Mail center each day to receive instruction?
___ I would like to be an area coordinator
___ I would like to be a local coordinator
___ I can do far more than that. I could devote full/half time to this work.
___ I am a pastor, deacon, or other leader of a church. I believe that I can persuade our entire church to become involved in this action.
___ I am a leader in a non-church organization (Rotary, YMCA, Optimists, Boys' Club, etc.). I believe I can persuade our organization to back this action.
___ I have made copies of this form and will encourage my friends, fellow church members, and co-workers to send it to you, also.
Other comments, ideas, or questions:
_____
_____
_____

Please fill in the form on the reverse side and mail to:

Coalition for the Code
P.O. Box 3086
Santa Fe Springs, CA 90670

Please remember to make copies and mail or give to friends, family, and associates at work, in your neighborhood, at church or to other groups.